D1165390

We Were Always Free

WE WERE ALWAYS FREE

The Maddens of
Culpeper County, Virginia,
A 200-Year Family History

T.O. MADDEN, JR.

with Ann L. Miller

Foreword by Nell Irvin Painter

W. W. NORTON & COMPANY
New York   London

Photograph research and preparation by Stephen W. Sylvia

Library of Congress Cataloging-in-Publication Data
Madden, T. O.
    We were always free : The Maddens of Culpeper County,
Virginia; A 200-year family history /
T. O. Madden, Jr., with Ann L. Miller.
        p.   cm.
    Includes bibliographical references (p.   ) and index.
    1. Madden family.   2. Afro-Americans—Virginia—Biography.
3. Virginia—Biography.   I. Miller, Ann L., 1954–   .   II. Title.
E185.96.M18   1992
975.5'00496073022—dc20
[B]   91-30200

ISBN 0-393-03347-3

W.W. Norton & Company, Inc.
500 Fifth Avenue, New York, N.Y. 10110
W.W. Norton & Company Ltd.
10 Coptic Street, London WC1A 1PU

1 2 3 4 5 6 7 8 9 0

Dedicated to

Sarah Madden (1758–1824)
and
Willis Madden (1799–1879)

CONTENTS

CONTENTS

FOREWORD

꒰꒱

Nell Irvin Painter

The Madden family of Virginia is an unusual clan of Americans in that they are people of mixed African and European descent who, through law, luck, and enormous hard work and enterprise, escaped the awful fate of so many others like themselves. Never enslaved, the Madden family made its way twice to relative prosperity and standing. T. O. Madden, Jr., who presents the narrative that follows, built on the ruins of his great-grandfather's tavern business, which was weakened by economic change and ruined by the Civil War. T. O. Madden, Jr., looks back to a proud genealogy, but he is a self-made man.

The voice in this narrative, which speaks in the first person singular throughout, belongs to him, a living person, now eighty-eight years old. *We Were Always Free* is, in fact, autobiography. As an old man's life narrative, it justifies his choices, rectifies his actions along lines of larger historical tradition, and fashions an appropriate identity. As autobiography, it concentrates on the figures who engender identity.

Nell Irvin Painter is Edwards Professor of History at Princeton University.

How American is this search for identity! and, given the prominence, even the very insistence on the term *free* through which Madden frames his identity, how very *Negro* American! In *We Were Always Free*, Madden relates who he is and who his people were, pointing to a more enduring and less contingent self than the self-made man of Chapter Nine. Like so many of the stories that Amerians tell themselves to establish who they are, this one posits both who the Maddens were and what they were not. Free Negro Virginians, they were never slaves. Madden's title proclaims that the United States has a history of enslavement and that enslavement still counts in American identity. This, then, is a narrative of family history and the definition of a twentieth-century self.

A FREE NEGRO FAMILY OF VIRGINIA

Like many other southern free Negro families originating in the colonial era (when many whites, women as well as men, were subject to servitude), the family of T. O. Madden, Jr., began with the birth in 1758 of his great-great-grandmother Sarah Madden. She is one of the two ancestors to whom he dedicates this book. Sarah was the first free person of color in this family, although Sarah's mother, Mary Madden, contributed the surname that endured. Mary Madden was an Irishwoman who had probably immigrated as a servant a few years before Sarah's birth. Although the myths of Virginia would make every colonial who was white into an aristocrat, Mary Madden, like most other eighteenth-century Virginians, was indigent. But unlike many others, she was free. Of Sarah Madden's father, nothing is known.

The legal definition of mixed-race children of blacks and whites had been settled in 1662, when the Virginia legislature enacted laws prohibiting interracial marriages and declaring that children followed the status of their mother. Such legislation made children like Sarah Madden free, but illegitimate. The legislators of Virginia, who came disproportionately from the Tidewater gentry, seem to have been particularly offended by the idea—and the frequent reality—that English or white men and women would be intimate with blacks or Indians, for they reenacted punitive laws on such cases in 1696, 1705, 1753, and 1765, the last two of which Madden mentions in regard to his great-great-grandmother's indenture. Punishments under law fell heaviest on white women who bore the children of Negro men and lightest on white men who impregnated women of any color.[1]

Despite a common assumption (which springs from nine-teenth-century practices in the Lower South) that race mixing occurred mainly at the instigation of wealthy white male planters who imposed themselves on their female slaves, this was not the origin of most mulattoes and free Negroes in the Upper South, which, of course, includes Virginia. During the colo-nial era most of the rather small proportion of Virginia's Negro population that was free was descended from very poor whites, women as well as men.[2] Miscegenation began as soon as Euro-peans, Indians, and Africans encountered one another in Vir-ginia in the seventeenth century. By the eighteenth century the Indians who remained in Virginia had virtually disap-peared as a separate group, absorbed into populations increas-ingly identified as either white or Negro. As would be the case in other American regions within and without the South, the use of biracial terminology came to obscure the presence of

[1]James Hugo Johnston, *Race Relations in Virginia and Miscegenation in the South, 1776–1860* (Amherst: University of Massachusetts Press, 1970), pp. 166–73. A. Leon Higginbotham, Jr., *In the Matter of Color: Race and the American Legal Pro-cess: The Colonial Period* (New York: Oxford University Press, 1978), pp. 40–45.

[2]James Hugo Johnson, *Race Relations in Virginia and Miscegenation in the South, 1776–1860* (Amherst: University of Massachusetts Press, 1970), pp. 177–81; John Hope Franklin, *The Free Negro in North Carolina, 1790–1860* (Chapel Hill: Uni-versity of North Carolina Press, 1943), pp. 38–39; Joel Williamson, *New People: Miscegenation and Mulattoes in the United States* (New York: Free Press, 1980), pp. 14–15, 25, 31; Winthrop D. Jordan, *White over Black: American Attitudes toward the Negro, 1550–1812* (Chapel Hill: University of North Carolina Press, 1968), pp. 137–38; Martha Elizabeth Hodes, "Sex across the Color Line: White Women and Black Men in the Nineteenth-Century American South," unpublished Ph.D. dissertation, Princeton University, 1991, pp. 2–3.

people descended from Indians. It is not possible to discern the proportion of eighteenth-century white and Negro Virginians of Indian descent, although it must have been substantial among those who had been in Virginia more than one or two generations, particularly among Negroes.

Thanks to what now appears as extraordinary openness of racial and economic status in the seventeenth century, Negroes could become free through a variety of means besides having a mother who was free. They could, for instance, work out their indentures or purchase their own freedom. By the late seventeenth century, however, the racial-economic regime hardened. After 1682 enslavement for life became the rule for Africans and people of African descent, making it virtually impossible for Negroes who had been servants in Virginia to become free after serving a given number of years. By the eighteenth century the legislature had systematized slavery into a racial institution, in which most Virginians of African descent were permanently condemnded to slavery and most Euro-Virginians would ultimately become free.[3]

Once working one's way out of servitude became extraordinary for Negroes, free parentage remained as the main avenue to freedom. This meant that between 1700 and 1782 (when manumission was made easier), most Negroes who were born free were descended at some point from Europeans. Within the Negro population of eighteenth-century Virginia, free Negroes like Sarah Madden would have been exceptional for being relatively light-skinned as well as for being free. But people like Sarah Madden were not exceptional in other ways. If their color and status set them apart, their economic situation did not. They were quite ordinary for being poor, for poverty was a status in which they had a good deal of company: slaves, who were the poorest of the southern poor; poor

---

[3]John H. Russell, *The Free Negro in Virginia, 1619–1865,* Johns Hopkins University Studies in Historical and Political Science, v. XXXI (Baltimore: Johns Hopkins Press, 1913), p. 39. The case of Anthony Johnson, a prosperous Negro freeman in seventeenth-century Virginia, exemplifies the relative flexibility of race relations before about 1700. See T. H. Breen and Stephen Innes, *"Myne Owne Ground": Race and Freedom on Virginia's Eastern Shore, 1640–1676* (New York: Oxford University Press, 1980).

and indentured whites like Mary Madden; and the poor who were free, whether black, white, or brown. At the same time, while Sarah Madden was working off her indenture, she and her free Negro peers were relatively few in number in Virginia.

According to 1782 estimates by St. George Tucker, then a professor at the College of William and Mary, later one of Virginia's most renowned judges, there were between eighteen hundred and twenty-eight hundred free Negroes in Virginia. In that year a law was passed allowing masters to emancipate slaves in their wills, a provision that seems to have led to a significant increase in the numbers of free Negroes. Tucker did not enumerate whites, so the first reliable eighteenth-century numbers come from the federal census.

In 1790, when Sarah Madden had just finished her thirty-one-year indenture and when the first federal census was taken, Virginia's population included 12,766 free Negroes, representing 4.2 percent of the Negro population as a whole. At the same time there were 293,427 slaves and 442,115 whites (indentured and free) in Virginia.[4] Although the free Negro population grew significantly in the early nineteenth century, the postrevolutionary era had seen the largest rate of increase of free Negroes until the end of the Civil War, almost four generations later.

With social, legal, and economic practices stacked against them, most free Negroes remained impoverished. Considering the paltry sums that even skilled women earned for their work, it is not surprising that among free people, women of color were at the bottom of the economic hierarchy. In Sarah Madden's case, however, financial frugality and business acumen defied the rule. Once she was free, Madden made her living and supported her family in Culpeper County through virtually the only skilled occupations open to free women of color:

---

[4] Ira Berlin, *Slaves without Masters: The Free Negro in the Antebellum South* (New York: Pantheon, 1974), pp. 6–9, 46–48, 396–98, and Russell, p. 10. See also Higginbotham, p. 59. In 1806 Tucker, sitting on the Virginia Court of Appeals, decided the case of *Hudgins v. Wright* on the ground that Negroes were assumed to be enslaved unless they could prove they were free.

dressmaking and laundering. She managed to accumulate enough personal property, notably cattle and chickens, to go into business. Even as an old woman she regularly sold eggs.

Women like Sarah Madden were to be found among the tiny minority of free Negroes in the Upper South who managed to gain property. If the case of Petersburg, Virginia, is any indication, as a female head of household Sarah Madden also belonged to a sizable group that represented about half of the free Negro families in towns. In Petersburg, too, free Negro women were likely not to be married, even though they headed households and had children. Here the law foreclosed their chances, for slaves could not marry, and interracial marriages were also out of bounds.[5]

Despite her unremitting hard work and her ability to purchase domestic animals and support her family, Sarah Madden remained poor and unschooled throughout her life. Her family is justly proud that poverty did not extinguish her commitment to her children or her bravery when the unity of her family was threatened. In 1783 she traveled some fifty miles without a pass, although the open roads were not considered any woman's territory. Madden appealed to Judge James Mercer to keep her children from being sold away, an appeal that seems to have been mostly in vain. Interestingly enough, in this extraordinarily courageous act Sarah Madden was not unique. Although it is not possible to ascertain how many slave mothers turned to the judicial system for the protection of their children, it is clear that Madden anticipated a similar feat some thirty years later on the part of the woman whom Americans know as Sojourner Truth. While still a slave in New York State, Truth traveled the roads of Ulster County and went to court to regain custody of her youngest child, who had been sold into perpetual slavery in the South illegally.[6]

[5] Lebsock, pp. 89–90, 97–98, 103–104. Russell overlooks the free Negroes who earned their own title to real property, ascribing their landholding to bequests from their former owners, p. 149.

[6] [Olive Gilbert and Frances Titus], *The Narrative of Sojourner Truth: A Bondswoman of Olden Time* . . . (Battle Creek, Mich.: Sojourner Truth, 1878), pp. 44–54.

Sarah Madden's son Willis Madden, born in 1799, is the
second central (and fatherless) character in the historical
section of T. O. Madden, Jr.'s story. Like this mother, Willis Madden emerges from these pages as a versatile, hardworking entrepreneur of impeccable integrity. Just as his
mother had employed her every competence, so Willis
Madden became a skilled cobbler, blacksmith, distiller,
teamster, and tavern keeper in the early nineteenth century. Like his mother, Willis Madden could not benefit from
schooling, yet he acquired considerable real and personal
property and built up a diversified business. If ever two
people deserved to be called "hardworking" and "enterpris-
ing," they were Sarah and Willis Madden, and these quali-
ties earned them the dedication of this book. Such Madden
attributes seemed not overly to have impressed their fellow
white Virginians, who denigrated the character of the entire
group to which the Maddens belonged. Throughout Sarah
and Willis Madden's active lives—which stretched from the
mid-eighteenth through the mid-nineteenth century—white
Virginians continually cast aspersions of the worthiness of
free Negroes to remain in their native state. This was the
case in neighboring Upper South states as well. Again and
again, petitions to the legislature—two of which came from
the Maddens' own Culpeper County—maligned free Negroes
as a public burden that should be forcibly expelled. While
Sarah Madden was sewing and washing and milking and
churning butter, her wealthy neighbor to the west, Thomas
Jefferson, was calling people like her "pests in society" and
declaring them to be incapable of taking care of themselves
or their children.[7] Hedged about by legal and societal pro-
hibitions, free Negroes tried to survive in a society increas-

[7]Thomas Jefferson, 1814, quoted in Russell, p. 75. Petitions, by Virginia county,
1790–1851, in which free Negro Virginians are termed burdens, are mentioned
in Johnston, pp. 58–59. From North Carolina, petitions from 1796 to 1831 are
notes in Franklin, pp. 21, 68–69, 101.

ingly tailored to the needs of the wealthy who owned the people who worked for them. While free Negroes worked incessantly in order to scape by, wealthy whites advocated what they termed colonization, by which they meant expulsion and forcible settlement in West Africa.

Such inconsiderate attitudes as Jefferson's signaled a hardening of racial mores in the nineteenth century that was reflected in the declining rate of growth of free Negroes in the population of Virginia. In 1806 the Virginia legislature passed a law requiring adults who had been manumitted to leave the state within twelve months (children might remain in Virginia until their coming of age). However, the law did not specify a place where the manumitted might go, and nonslaveholding states and territories did not welcome the presence of freed Negro Virginians. This lack of refuge blunted the law's actual effect, for those who had been recently manumitted petitioned for permission to stay put. But the law nonetheless indicated an official willingness to curb the growth of the free Negro population that had long-range effects.[8]

Whereas the increase of free Negroes from 1810 to 1820 had been 20.7 percent, and from 1820 to 1830 had been 28.4 percent, after 1830 this growth slowed dramatically. From 1830 to 1840 the increase was 5.3 percent; from 1840 to 1850, 9.0 percent; and from 1850 to 1860, 6.8 percent.[9] Such stagnation reflected the increasing ability of large slaveholders to dominate the economy and the politics of the southern states. In Virginia, Negro codes became stricter in the aftermath of Gabriel Prosser's planned insurrection in 1800 and Nat Turner's revolt in 1831.

Not only did gaining freedom become more difficult, but free Negroes had to perform an ever-tenser balancing act

[8] Russell, pp. 68–71.
[9] The proportion of Negroes who were free in Virginia was 8.0 percent in 1820, 10.0 percent in 1840, and 10.6 percent in 1860. Berlin, pp. 135–37.

between survival and freedom.[10] In T. O. Madden, Jr.'s
narrative, these imperatives appear most poignantly in the
1823 testimonials to Willis Madden's good character and
solvency, which made it possible for the family to remain
together after his sister Mariah gave birth to a child she
could not support.[11] In a land meant more and more to hold
only enslaved Negroes and free whites, the space for free
Negroes continually narrowed. In the 1850s that space grew
tighter, but with contradictory results.[12]

On the one hand, political rhetoric in the 1850s heated
up against free blacks throughout the South. The defenders
of slavery redoubled their claims that free Negroes were
idle and vicious and demanded they be forcibly deported.
White workingmen demanding the imposition of ever-greater
occupational restrictions on the men and women they saw
as all-too-successful economic competitors. Advocates of
slavery-as-a-positive-good declared that slavery, rather than
freedom, represented the ideal status for workers. In 1856
the Virginia legislature passed a law providing for the vol-
untary enslavement of free Negroes—a measure that found
only three takers. The United States Supreme Court's *Dred
Scott v. Sandford* decision, which in 1857 declared that
Negroes could not be citizens and had no civil rights, gave
further impetus to the movement to expel Negroes who were
not slaves.[13] Within the realms of public discourse and law,
the 1850s were a decade of vicious opposition to free Negroes,
in Virginia and the United States generally.

[10] The Madden narrative does not mention the violence that free Negroes in
Virginia often suffered and that appears in the autobiography of Willis Augustus
Hodges. See Willard B. Gatewood, Jr., *Free Man of Color: The Autobiography of
Willis Augustus Hodges* (Knoxville: University of Tennessee Press, 1982), pp. 25–
35, 64–73.

[11] These testimonials are on pages 50–54.

[12] Ira Berlin, the historian of free Negroes in the South, entitles one chapter
on the 1850s "The Best of Times, the Worst of Times."

[13] Berlin, pp. 362–75, Russell, pp. 108–9, Franklin, pp. 211–21.

On the other hand, the 1850s were a time of prosperity (discounting the panic of 1857) that also benefited free Negroes.[14] In the present story of the Madden family, Willis Madden achieved his greatest success in the late 1840s and early 1850s. These were the years after he had built his new home, paid off his mortgage, and become able to employ several of his relatives in his tavern, campground, hauling, and farming businesses. These were also the years before the Orange and Alexandria Railroad began diverting traffic and hence clientele away from the Chinquapin Neck crossroads where Madden's tavern was situated.

During the height of his prosperity Willis Madden had his photograph taken and acquired personal luxuries (a clock, for instance, that T. O. Madden, Jr., still owns) that marked him as a man of stature. This was fitting, according to T. O. Madden, Jr., because Willis Madden was the wealthiest free Negro in his area, a man of standing who appeared at court and received letters that addressed him as "Sir." In southern terms, Willis Madden had achieved the status of an honorable man, which made him highly unusual as a Negro. Just as the word *free* implies existence of the status of slave, so the concept of *honorable* is meant in white parlance to stand in opposition to that of the common run of Negro. For in the United States after the late seventeenth century, *Negro* and *slave* were practically synonymous, and *slaves had no recognized honor*. Considering this symbolic history, T. O. Madden, Jr.'s stress on the respect that his great-grandfather enjoyed among gentlemen is perfectly understandable. In addition, the association of honor with maleness also underscores his pride in an upstanding ancestor who was male, an ancestor in addition to Sarah Madden.

As the first male in what T. O. Madden, Jr., identifies as his ancestral line (Mary Madden and Sarah Madden to Willis Madden), Willis was also the first to marry, which was

[14] Berlin, pp. 343–45.

also an indication of his level of respectability. As befitted a free Negro of standing, his wife was also free, and lighter-skinned than he. The Willis Maddens, like free Negroes elsewhere in Virginia and the Upper South, kept company with other free Negroes, forming what historian John Hope Franklin has called a caste within a caste. Franklin adds that the free Negro caste was often looked down upon by black slaves as well as whites, but this would hardly have been the case with the family of Willis Madden, thanks to obvious wealth and enterprise.[15]

Until well into the nineteenth century, the Maddens lacked access to one of the main perquisites of respectability—literacy. In this regard they were typical of free Negroes, who were systematically barred from securing an education. In 1850 less than 17 percent of free Negroes in Virginia could read and write.[16] For free Negroes of Willis Madden's generation, illiteracy represented an unfortunately common fact of life. Similarly, the Madden family would have found it difficult to remain practicing Negro Baptists, once black men were prohibited from preaching after the Nat Turner Rebellion of 1831. For all intents and purposes, both education and a Baptist church of their own would have to wait until after the Civil War.

The Civil War provides one of the most intriguing chapters in the history of the Madden family, one that T. O. Madden, Jr., treats as tragedy with all the irony intact. During the armed struggle against slavery the family was practically ruined, a defeat from which his great-grandfather never completely recovered, psychologically or financially. The source of Willis Madden's wealth, the key to his identity as an independent, free man, was his tavern, which had the misfortune of sitting directly in the path of advanc-

[15] Franklin, pp. 163–64.
[16] Russell, p. 145.

ing and retreating armies, Union and Confederate. Repeated wartime deprivation stripped Madden's tavern and farm of animals and provisions, inflicting nearly twenty-five hundred dollars' worth of damage, an enormous sum in those days. The war that made all the Negroes in Virginia free broke Willis Madden. Not until March 1873 did the federal government finally reimburse him a sum that was less than nine hundred dollars. This was enough to pay his debts and to create discord within the family, but not sufficient to rebuild his business. Willis Madden's depression, decline, and death mark the end of Chapter Seven and the end of the family history as passed down through documents and family lore. The next chapter begins T. O. Madden, Jr.'s own memoir, beginning with the story of his father, T. O. Madden, Jr.

Thomas Obed ("T.O.") Madden, Sr., born in 1860, was the illegitimate child of Willis's daughter Maria and a white man whose identity has never been settled conclusively. Coming of age after the Civil War, T.O. found his options were far wider than those of his forebears, an indication of the degree to which the antebellum system of slavery had restricted the opportunities of Negroes who were free as well as those who were enslaved. T.O. learned to read and write, attended a Baptist church that his grandfather had founded on his own land, and traveled outside Virginia. As the first generation of a free family to grow up in an era of freedom, he switched occupations and finally settled on one, teaching, that had been illegal in his grandfather's time.

The precariousness of T. O. Madden's job as a teacher is not related simply to race: Southern schools—Virginia schools in particular—for whites as well as Negroes were notoriously underfunded, and white as well as Negro teachers competed for a limited number of positions.[17] At the same

[17]James D. Anderson, *The Education of Blacks in the South, 1860–1935* (Chapel Hill: University of North Carolina Press, 1988), p. 101.

time, Madden's experience had a clear racial edge. Through-out the South during the long era of segregation, Negro schools were in session for less time than white, and Negro teachers earned far less than their white counter-parts. Madden's lack of money, even while both he and his wife were fully employed as teachers, was characteristic of southern Negro teachers, who though relatively well paid among Negroes, routinely sought additional employment to make ends meet.

Madden ad his wife taught and farmed and worked their children as farm laborers. The Madden parents thereby for-feited their children's education to ensure their economic well-being, a choice that T. O. Madden, Jr., still resents. T. O. Madden, Jr., accuses his father of purposefully sac-rificing his children so that he could continue to teach. That such a choice was necessary is an indication of the precar-iousness of southern Negro class formation in the era of segregation.

T. O. Madden, Jr., says that his schooling stopped when he was big enough to plow. Had he not been of such enter-prising temperament, he might not have achieved the middle-class status of his father or the wealth of his great-grandfa-ther, for the ranks of his eleven siblings, while mostly middle class, include some workers. Like many other Negro fami-lies in the early twentieth century, the younger Maddens were as liable to suffer downward as to achieve upward mobility. They were fortunate in that their parents could educate them at home, even when they missed formal schooling in order to work.

Madden was doubly fortunate that his farm lay within reach of a large urban market: Washington, D.C.[18] Else-where in the 1930s South truck farming was limited by the very rurality of the society, in which large markets were

---

[18]Jack Temple Kirby, *Rural Worlds Lost: The American South, 1920–1960* (Baton Rouge: Louisiana State University Press, 1987), pp. 40, 41.

seldom so accessible. Madden was also lucky to be able to farm his own land, for throughout the twentieth century increasing numbers of southern farmers, Negro and white, farmed as landless tenants and sharecroppers. Even though the policies of the New Deal and Fair Deal tended to move tenants and sharecroppers off the land, Madden, a land-owner, was able to remain on his own place. He began using a tractor relatively early among southern farmers, switching from horses in the late 1920s instead of the 1940s or 1950s.

Madden made much of his wealth through the sale of land that now lies within the greater Washington area. In this sense he has profited from the development of Washington, D.C., and of Virginia generally. While states like Mississippi, Louisiana, and Alabama still remain dismally poor, Virginia and Florida stand out among southern states for nonsouthern levels of wealth. As T. O. Madden, Jr.'s family history ends in wealth, it is still rooted in Virginia. This is no longer the Virginia in which his ancestors had to make their way through the interstices of a punitive system, but a prosperous and desegregated postwar Virginia in which land in the northern part of the state is well worth selling.

At the end—in fact, by the middle—of this family story, the key word of the title, *free*, no longer has the resonance supplied by *slave*. By the second half of the twentieth century the fact that this Negro family owns land in the part of Virginia that is developed becomes as crucial—though unstressed—as the family's long history. T. O. Madden, Jr., is a wealthy man who has written a family history that defines his identity as an individual, as a Negro, and as a Virginian. It is a narrative shaped by personal as well as historical imperatives.

PREFACE

and Note to the Reader

We have always been free.

Though we have sometimes been servants, sometimes laborers, no member of our family has ever been a slave.

Like most other Negro families, we had our family history, stories to tell, passed down through the generations, but like others, we had little proof or documentation for these stories.

For more than a century the only Madden family documents that we knew of consisted of a collection of bills and receipts kept by my great-grandfather Willis Madden, a farmer and tavernkeeper who had built our house in eastern Culpeper County, Virginia, before the Civil War. The family kept these papers as curiosities, and they lay, half forgotten, in the attic since Willis Madden's death.

Soon after my father's death in 1949, something—perhaps curiosity about our past, a desire to know bygone generations now that my father was gone—made me want to see these papers for myself. They were still in the attic, hidden under the eaves in the hidebound trunk where Willis Madden had put them. Most of the papers, as I took them out, were nothing more than I had been told: bills, promises to pay, and receipts. But there were also other

papers—papers that made my hand shake and brought tears
to my eyes: letters, "free papers," birth records, the beginning of a documentation of our family that I never dreamed
existed, dating back to the middle of the eighteenth century.

That day my long-dead ancestors spoke to me. In the
forty years since I first opened the trunk, I've collected other
papers and stories, from family and friends and from more
official sources. Out of these, I have tried to reconstruct my
family's story. The documentation and the family legends
to follow do not tell this family's story as much as let my
ancestors speak for themselves. The story of the Madden
family is unusually complete in American Negro history,
and I owe it to my forebears—and to their future generations—to let them tell their own story.

Outstanding among my early family, and central to this
story, were my great-great-grandmother Sarah Madden and
her son Willis Madden, my great-grandfather. Sarah Madden, a woman alone and born a pauper, overcame many
obstacles—poverty, illiteracy, prejudice—to build a profit-
able business, keep her family together, and provide for them,
all against the odds. Willis Madden, who inherited his
mother's strength and determination, grew up to succeed at
a business that was largely closed to Negroes. No one gave
Willis Madden anything but a chance, but with that, and
through his own intelligence, ability, and effort, he became
a successful businessman and a respected member of the
community.

My history continues with chapters on some of the heirs
of Sarah and Willis Madden: Willis's daughter Maria, her
son Thomas Obed (my father), and his children. It is my
hope that you, my readers, will find the story of the Madden family interesting and even inspiring. And that these
very special Maddens of the past will live on in your
remembrance.

Some family documents, census records, and notes on other children of Sarah Madden are included as appendices. If they or any other part of this book answer some family research questions of other Maddens out there, I can only say: Cousins, I welcome you.

Much of this book is built upon original documents, many of which I found in Sarah Madden's trunk in the attic in 1949. Because it would have been awkward to transcribe all of them as a part of the text, I have chosen in many cases to summarize or quote portions in the text and to translate the entire document in a separate appendix.

Throughout this book I refer to my family as Negroes. This was the term I grew up with, and I still think it's the best description. As a look at any of the Madden family will tell you, we're no more "black" than we are "white." And I think that we're too far from Africa, and of mixed blood for too many generations, to be Afro- (or African-) American.

"Negro," "colored," and "person of color" were the terms of respect in my time and the times of my ancestors, and I have used them as such in this book. As a boy, growing up in the era of Jim Crow, I can't begin to tell you what an insult it was to call a Negro, especially another Negro, "black." We all knew what it was short for: "black nigger." There wasn't a worse thing you could say.

Different terms may be in fashion today, but they were not at the time most of this book takes place. I have used the old terms of description and respect, the ones that I— and my ancestors—knew and were comfortable with.

T. O. Madden, Jr.
Maddenville Farm
Elkwood, Virginia

INTRODUCTION

꒰꒱

Government in eighteenth-century Virginia, where this
story begins, was modeled on the English system.
Each county had a sheriff and a county court with its
"gentlemen justices," who sat as judges and had other
administrative and legal duties. Before the Revolution, the
Anglican Church (Church of England), the official or
"established" church, was also a major factor in Virginia's
government. Both the church and the secular government
were supported by taxes levied for that purpose. The vestry, or church officers of each parish (parish boundaries
usually corresponded to county lines), were persons of
influence who in many cases held positions in the county
government as well. Besides overseeing the functions of the
church, the vestry aided in the prosecution of certain legal
cases (including those involving sexual crimes, illegitimacy,
public profanity, drunkenness, and debts to the church).
The vestry was also responsible for the care of paupers and
of orphaned, neglected, or bastard children. Legal matters
relating to such cases were handled by the churchwardens—members of the vestry chosen for this work, who
acted in company with the local courts.

Paupers were cared for in the parish where they lived;
this was seen as a Christian duty. The very young, the old,

and the sick were cared for in private homes, and the hosts were paid for their time and expenses by the vestry. Paupers who were able to work were sent to the parish workhouse, where they were required to work at various jobs such as spinning, weaving, or leatherworking in return for their support. Those who refused to enter a workhouse, or to work there, could be refused further support by the parish; the alternative might be to starve.

Morals cases and the care of bastard children were items frequently found on the churchwardens' agendas. The colonial government had many laws concerning sexual conduct and misconduct. Sex outside marriage, interracial sex, having a bastard child—the list of punishable crimes went on, with sentences ranging from fines or public whippings to imprisonment and forced labor. Unwed mothers were subjected to heavy fines, which were increased if a white woman's child showed evidence of Negro blood. (The latter cases were fairly common. The eighteenth century was a status-conscious age. Women without money or good family names behind them often had difficulty finding husbands, and a number of these women formed relationships with free Negroes or slaves.)

As slaves could not legally marry, the laws—and punishments—were naturally applied only to free women. Even then they were seldom enforced against free Negroes but were mainly applied to white women. If the mother could not pay the fine and could not prove that she was able to support the child, the baby would be taken away.

Bastard children, as well as children whose families could not support them, were routinely taken from their mothers and given over—"bound out" or "indentured"—to someone willing to care for, train, and, in some cases, educate them until they became adults. If a mother could not pay the fine involved, she, too, was bound out as a servant for several years, with the money from the sale of her indenture applied toward the fine she owed. Mulatto children—children of mixed Negro and white ancestry (a 1705 Virginia statute defined a mulatto as "the child, grandchild or great-grandchild of a negro" with the corresponding proportion of white blood)—did not have to be educated, only taught to do some sort of useful work during the terms of their indentures. For much of the colonial period, too, they served longer than white children, but still, they were only servants, not slaves.

A child bound out by county and church officials was commonly indentured as a "servant and apprentice," a combination of an *indentured servant* (a person legally bound by a contract, or indenture, to work for a master for a definite term of years) and an *apprentice* (an individual, usually a child or teenager, indentured to serve a master until a certain age, usually eighteen or twenty-one, and in return taught a trade or useful occupation). A child bound out as a "servant and apprentice" would be cared for until he or she reached maturity and would be taught a means of earning a living.

Although many southerners euphemistically referred to their slaves as "servants," there was, legally, a great difference between a slave and a servant or apprentice. Servants and apprentices were under the control of their masters during their terms of indenture, and indentures could be bought and sold, but a servant could still own property and had many legal rights. Most important, the terms of indentured servants were due to end at some point, after which these individuals, and their children, would be free citizens. Servants were said to be "bound out" or "sold" into servitude, but actually it was the *indenture*, not the *servant*, that was sold. There was a world of difference between this and the situation of slaves: The sale of a slave meant actual ownership of that person, and that person's descendants, for life.

The bastard children who were bound out as servants were, of course, those who had free status. By law, all children—white, Negro, or mulatto—were slave or free according to the status of their mothers. No matter who the father was, the children of a slave woman would be slaves, while those of a free woman would be free. Interracial marriages were outlawed by the early eighteenth century, but the mulatto population continued to increase. Most of these were children of white men and female slaves, and these children were also slaves, blending back into the slave population. But a number of mulattoes were the offspring of free Negroes and free mulattoes, or of Negro or mulatto fathers and white mothers, and these children of free mothers were free, as were their descendants.

Free Negroes and mulattoes, some born free, some freed from slavery, formed a subculture in the South before the Civil War, accounting for about 10 percent of the entire Negro population. These "free persons of color" were feared and considered threats and subversives. On one hand, they were seen as dangerously skilled and ambitious tradesmen and craftsmen, in competition with slave labor and white businesses. On the other hand (and often simultaneously), they were depicted in the popular imagination and press as debased, lazy individuals, burdens to society, criminals, and rallying points for slave rebellions. They were intimidated, restricted by law, and discriminated against, but they survived, and endured, and among their numbers were many of the free workers, farmers, skilled craftsmen, and small businessmen of antebellum Virginia.

This is the story of one of those families.

We Were Always Free

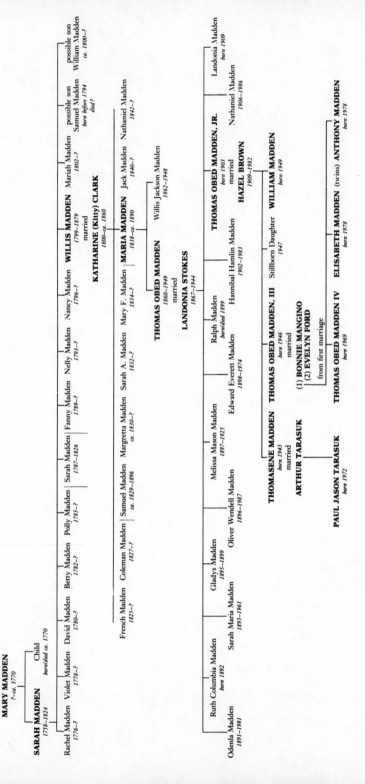

MARY MADDEN
?–ca. 1770

Child
born/died ca. 1770

SARAH MADDEN
1758–1824

Rachel Madden
1776–?

Violet Madden
1778–?

David Madden
1780–?

Betty Madden
1782–?

Polly Madden
1785–?

Sarah Madden
1787–1826

Fanny Madden
1789–?

Nelly Madden
1793–?

Nancy Madden
1796–?

WILLIS MADDEN
1799–1879
married
KATHARINE (Kitty) CLARK
1800–ca. 1860

Mariah Madden
1802–?

possible son
Samuel Madden
born before 1794
died ?

possible son
William Madden
ca. 1800–?

French Madden
1825–?

Coleman Madden
1827–?

Samuel Madden
ca. 1829–1896

Margretta Madden
ca. 1830–?

Sarah A. Madden
1832–?

Mary F. Madden
1834–?

MARIA MADDEN
1838–ca. 1890

Jack Madden
1840–?

Nathaniel Madden
1842–?

THOMAS OBED MADDEN
1860–1949
married
LANDONIA STOKES
1867–1944

Willis Jackson Madden
1862–1948

Odenia Madden
1891–1981

Ruth Columbia Madden
born 1892

Sarah Maria Madden
1893–1961

Gladys Madden
1895–1899

Oliver Wendell Madden
1896–1987

Melissa Mason Madden
1897–1925

Edward Everett Madden
1898–1974

Ralph Madden
born/died 1899

Hannibal Hamlin Madden
1902–1983

THOMAS OBED MADDEN, JR.
born 1903
married
HAZEL BROWN
1909–1982

Nathaniel Madden
1906–1986

Landonia Madden
born 1909

Stillborn Daughter
1947

WILLIAM MADDEN
born 1949

THOMASENE MADDEN
born 1943
married
ARTHUR TARASUK

THOMAS OBED MADDEN, III
born 1946
married
(1) BONNIE MANGINO
(2) EVELYN FORD
from first marriage

ELISABETH MADDEN (twins) ANTHONY MADDEN
born 1978   born 1978

PAUL JASON TARASUK
born 1972

THOMAS OBED MADDEN IV
born 1969

Chapter One

MARY MADDEN

WHEREAS some doubts have arisen whether children got by any Englishman upon a negro woman should be slave or Free. Be it therefore enacted and declared by this present grand assembly, that all children borne in this country shalbe held bond or free only according to the condition of the mother. And that if any christian shall committ Fornication with a negro man or woman, he or shee soe offending shall pay double the Fines imposed by the former act

Virginia statute, December 1662

AND be it further enacted by the authoritie aforesaid and it is hereby enacted, That if any English woman being free shall have a bastard child by any negro or mulatto, she pay the sume of fifteen pounds sterling, within one moneth [month] after such bastard child shall be born, to the Church wardens of the parish where she shall be delivered of such child, and in default of such payment she shall be taken into the possession of the said Church wardens and disposed of for five yeares, and the said fine of fifteen pounds, or whatever the woman shall be disposed of for, shall be paid, one third part to the majesties for and towards the support of the government and the contingent charges thereof, and one third part to the use of the parish where the offence is committed, and the other third part to the informer, and that such bastard child shall be bound out as a servant *by the said Church wardens untill he or she shall attaine the age of thirty years. . . .*

Virginia statute, April 1691

My great-great-grandmother Sarah Madden was born a mulatto bastard child in Spotsylvania County, Virginia, on August 4, 1758. Her mother, Mary Madden, a white woman, was a pauper living on public charity, without family or friends—and now marked as a white woman who had borne a child to a black man. Since her mother was a free woman, Sarah would at least be free also, but she would be a free Negro in a society where many would prefer her to be a slave.

We know almost nothing about Mary Madden's early life, and we may never know more. No known records tell where she was born, who her family was, or where she lived before she appeared, pregnant and alone, in Spotsylvania County in 1758. But through the generations the story was told that Mary Madden was an Irish girl who came to America in the 1750s. The Madden name was (and remains) a common one in Ireland, and Madden families there in the eighteenth century ranged from simple farmers and villagers to landed gentry, wealthy and important. There were also Madden families in Virginia as early as the seventeenth century (a Henry Madden died in Isle of Wight County around 1687), and there were other Maddens in Frederick, Fairfax, and Prince William counties in the eighteenth century, as well as a James Madden who died in Fredericksburg in 1793. However, there is no known evidence of Mary Madden's relationship to any of these families. She may have been a peasant, or an heiress, or someone in between. But whoever she was, she must have had what this old farmer calls "good blood" in her—strength, courage, and the will to survive— which she passed on to her descendants.

When Sarah was born, Mary Madden was living on the

2

Collins farm, in the branches of the Po River near the center of the county. Joseph Collins, owner of the seven-hundred-acre plantation, had died the year before, and Mary was in the care of Joseph's son, James Collins. Mary Madden was not there as a relative or friend but as a tenant—a charge of the county. As a pauper in need of medical attention she had been placed by the church vestry with a local family. At the end of the year the church vestry paid James Collins six hundred pounds of tobacco—legal money in colonial Virginia—"for maintaining Mary Madden & her child."

In February 1759 the vestry issued an order for various paupers, including Mary and Sarah, to report to the local workhouse the following October. In the workhouse the paupers were "to be Employed as the Law Directs"—put to work to help pay for their support. Their support was provided for by the parish levy, or tax, which was usually paid in tobacco, the main cash crop of the region. The 1759 order ended with a warning: "That all those Persons of the Poor who have Tobacco levied for them this present year . . . may not Depend on any further allowance from the Parish hereafter unless they Repare to the Workhouse."

So Mary went to the workhouse, taking her baby with her.

I can imagine Mary there, working daily at the loom or spinning wheel, with Sarah on the floor at her feet, playing with the bits of thread her mother dropped. But Mary also owed a fine for having Sarah, and since she could not pay it, according to law, she would have to work this off, too, by being sold as a servant. At the same time arrangements were being made for Sarah.

In April 1760 Sarah Madden, not quite two years old, was taken from her mother. Her destination, and new home, were the town of Fredericksburg. As the law provided, she had been bound out until the age of thirty-one, to become an indentured "Servant and Apprentice" to George Fraser,

3

In his great-great-grandmother Sarah's trunk, T. O. Madden, Jr., discovered a treasure trove of documents covering two hundred years of Madden family history. The hidebound trunk is lined with pages from a Salem, Massachusetts, newspaper dated March 24, 1820. Photo, Stephen W. Sylvia.

a merchant in that town. We don't know if Sarah ever saw her mother again.

As cruel as it seems today, the treatment of Mary and Sarah Madden was common for paupers and bastard children for the eighteenth and much of the nineteenth centuries. Mary and Sarah fared no better—and no worse—than others in the same situation. They had run afoul of laws deemed necessary for the care of the poor and the control of a variety of social problems: poverty, interracial relationships, illegitimacy, and the care of children whose families could not support them. Mary Madden was just one of a large number of similar women, just one face in a crowd, and like a face in a crowd, she disappears from view. The fate of Mary Madden is as unknown as most of the rest of her life. There is no sign of her in the church or county records for ten years after Sarah was taken to Fredericksburg. Then, in 1770, there is one last, brief mention—a note in the vestry book that Mary Turnley, wife of Francis Turnley, was paid ten shillings for "laying Mary Madden," apparently a reference to Mary Turnley's helping Mary Madden deliver another baby (ten shillings was the usual fee for assisting a woman in childbirth). Probably both Mary and the baby died soon after this, for there is no more mention of mother or child in the county or vestry records.

Chapter Two

SARAH MADDEN

꾸닞꾸

THIS INDENTURE Made the Seventeenth of April in the Year
of our Lord One thousand seven hundred and sixty Between Charles
Lewis & Richard Brooke Gentlemen Church Wardens of the Parish
of Saint George in the County of Spotsylvania of the one part and
George Fraser of the Town of Fredericksburg Merchant of the other
part WITNESSETH that whereas Mary Madden a free unmarried
white woman resident in the said Parish was upon the fourth Day of
August in the Year of our Lord One thousand seven hundred and
fifty Eight at the Parish and County aforesaid delivered of a Mulatto
female Bastard Child since Baptized and known by the name of Sarah
NOW THIS INDENTURE WITNESSETH that the said Charles
Lewis & Richard Brooke by virtue of their Office aforesaid and
according to the form of the Act of Assembly in that Case made and
provided have put and bound and by these presents do put and bind
the said female Mulatto Child known by the name of Sarah Maddin
unto him the said George Fraser his Executors Administrators or
Assigns as a Servant and Apprentice untill she be and arrive at the
full Age of Thirty one Years from the Day of the birth aforesaid, and
during all which time the said Sarah shall serve the said George Fraser
his Executor Administrators and Assigns truly faithfully and honestly shall obey all his or their lawful Commands and in every thing
behave herself as becomes a diligint and obedient Servant And the
said George Fraser in bhalf of himself his Executors Administrators
or Assigns doth hereby Covenant bargain and agree with the Church

Wardens aforesaid in behalf of the said Sarah that he the said George Fraser his Executors Administrators or Assigns shall and will during the whole term and time aforesaid find and provide for the said Sarah Meat Drink Lodging and Apparel suitable and necesary for her and at the Expiration of the said Term of Servitude shall pay her such freedom dues as are prescribed by the Act of Assembly aforesaid IN WITNESS whereof the parties to these presents have hereunto set their Hands and affixed their Seals the day and Year first above written Sealed and delivered

> *In the presence of*
> *Alex Waugh Jun.*   *Charles Lewis*
> *John Semple*   *Richard Brooke*
> *Joseph Jones*   *George Fraser*
>
> Sarah Madden's indenture of servitude, 1760

Fredericksburg stands at the fall line of the Rappahannock River, and in Sarah Madden's day the uppermost point of the river was navigable by oceangoing ships. The rapids at the fall line divided lower Virginia, the Tidewater, from the Piedmont, the upcountry, which stretched west to the distant Blue Ridge Mountains.

In 1760 Fredericksburg was a bustling town, one of the major ports in Virginia, and the center of commerce for a region that included all the upland area drained by the Rappahannock and portions of the Shenandoah Valley beyond the mountains. Nearly everyone in town made a living from trade. The streets were lined with a variety of buildings, public and private: shops, warehouses, merchants' offices, townhouses, taverns. And the streets themselves were filled with people, on foot, on horseback, with carts piled high with goods: local businessmen, workmen, sailors, new arrivals from Europe, slaves, and servants. Mixed among these were the traders, small farmers, and planters who came, some all the way from the upper Piedmont and from the mountains to the west, to buy and sell produce and sup-

This Indenture Made the Seven [...] April in the
Year of our Lord One thousand seven hundred and [...] Between
Charles Lewis & Richard Brooke Gentlemen Church Wardens of the Parish
of Saint George in the County of Spotsylvania of the one part and George Fraser
of the Town of Fredericksburgh Merchant of the other part Witnesseth
that whereas Mary Madden a free unmarried white [...] resident in the
said Parish [...] the fourth Day of August in the Year of our Lord One
thousand seven [...] fifty eight at the Parish and County aforesaid
delivered of a Mulatto female Bastard Child since Baptized and known by
the name of Sarah Now this Indenture Witnesseth that the
said Charles Lewis & Richard Brooke by virtue of their Office aforesaid and according to the form of the Act of Assembly in that Case made and provided
have put and bound [...] these presents do put and bind the said female Mulatto Child known by [...] Sarah [...] unto the said George Fraser
his Executors Administrators or Assigns as a Servant and Apprentice until she
be and arrive at the full age of Thirty one Years from the Day of the birth a-
foresaid, during all which time the said Sarah shall serve the said George Fraser
his Executors Administrators or Assigns truly faithfully and honestly shall
obey all his or their lawfull Commands and in every thing behave herself as
[...] said obedient servant and [...] find the said George Fraser in behalf of himself his Executors Administrators or Assigns doth
hereby Covenant bargain and agree with the Church Wardens aforesaid in behalf of the said Sarah that he the said George Fraser his Executors Administrators or Assigns shall and will during the whole term and time aforesaid find and provide for the said Sarah Meat Drink Lodging and Apparel suitable and [...] for her and at the Expiration of the said Term
of Servitude shall pay [...] such freedom dues as are prescribed by the Act

*Sarah Madden's indenture papers were among the most surprising documents dis-
covered by T. O. Madden, Jr., in his ancestor's weathered trunk in 1949.*

8

of Assembly &c.   In Witness whereof the parties to these presents
have hereunto set their Hands and affixed their seals the day and Year
first above written ~ — — — — — —

   Sealed and delivered   Charles Lewis
In presence off
Alex Waugh Jr
John Semple   by Geo. Frazer   Lawr. Brooke
Joseph Jones

                                           Roger Frazer

                         A true Copy

                              W Underwood C.V.

plies. In all this activity probably no one took much notice of the delivery of a small child to George Fraser's house. New people came to Fredericksburg daily, and Sarah's arrival, in the spring of 1760, was just one more new face.

Sarah's future looked far from bright: She faced nearly thirty years of hard work and a lifetime of prejudice. With Sarah came her indenture papers, the legal term for the bond that related the story of her birth and the burden of her servitude.

Sarah's new master, George Fraser, was a Scotsman by birth. Though he turned out to be an unsuccessful businessman, Fraser maintained business connections and partnerships with other local merchants; most were also of Scottish ancestry. Alexander Wright, James Strachan, James Hunter, all of Fredericksburg, and Andrew Shepherd, who lived some forty miles east in the little town of Orange Courthouse, the seat of the county of Orange, were his most active business associates. Their dealings extended through Spotsylvania and the surrounding counties, especially Orange and Culpeper, and reached as far as the Shenandoah Valley.

The exact location of George Fraser's residence remains uncertain, but soon after he acquired Sarah's indenture, he bought a one-third interest (with his partners at the time, Hunter and Wright) in lots 23 and 24, the half block bordered by Sophia, Caroline, and William streets, close to the wharves and warehouses along the river. This land was a prime location for a merchant's office and a sensible location for a merchant's dwelling. The Wrights apparently lived on the property, and the Frasers may have had a house there also, possibly living on the land as tenants before George Fraser purchased his interest in the lots.

It is known that the Frasers had a number of slaves, and Sarah was probably housed with them. Even when she was a small child, her training could soon have begun in domestic tasks, little jobs at first, then with more responsibility as she grew: helping tend the garden, cook, clean, and mend and wash clothes.

George Fraser died in early 1765, when Sarah was six. He left a personal estate of a little over four hundred pounds, including his eight slaves, furniture and household goods, and a few luxuries, such as silver teaspoons and imported china. Sarah, or Sally as the Frasers called her, was appraised along with the rest of his estate: "one Molatto Girl named Sall." As a young girl, a servant, not a slave, Sarah, or actually her indenture, was valued at only ten pounds, the same as George Fraser's horse and less than the value of the Frasers' best bedstead.

George Fraser's estate should have supported his widow and two daughters comfortably, except for the fact that he died deeply in debt. His troubles had begun several years earlier. In the early 1760s Fraser was involved in a "Negro concern"—slave trading—with several partners, including Colonel James Madison, a merchant and landowner of nearby Orange County. Overextended, Fraser had borrowed money and gotten credit from Colonel Madison. As his debt grew and his business floundered, he could neither pay Colonel Madison his share of the profits from the slave sales nor repay the money and credit he had borrowed.

By early 1763, two years before his death, his total debt stood at more than four hundred pounds. The half block and buildings that Fraser and his partners purchased had cost three hundred pounds only three years before. Given time, Fraser might have pulled himself out of debt, but time was something he was running out of; his health was failing. He made his will in late June 1763, and within two years he was dead, his debt unpaid.

James Madison was apparently a patient man. Fraser had promised, and failed, several times to pay the debt. After Fraser's death Madison tried to collect for two years. Of course, interest was also accumulating, so patience had potential profit. By late 1767, after repeated, and empty, promises from Fraser's widow, Colonel Madison's patience had worn thin. Esther Fraser was summoned to Orange Court, where the case of *Madison v. Fraser's Executrix* was settled by a jury and the gentleman justices—except for Colonel Madison, who had excused himself from the bench immediately before the case was to be heard, to reappear as plaintiff. Colonel Madison was awarded 407 pounds, plus costs. If the estate of George Fraser failed to satisfy the debt, the remainder was to come from the property that the widow had already inherited. The judgment amounted to more than the appraised value of Fraser's personal property. And although the sale of the one-third interest in the Caroline Street property could provide enough funds to save the Frasers from total disaster, many family possessions had to be sold or transferred to Colonel Madison to settle the debt.

Among the property transferred as a result of the judgment was nine-year-old Sarah Madden, still with twenty-two years of service remaining on her indenture. A copy of her papers was made out to Colonel Madison, and Sarah, either by herself or in company with some of the other property being transferred—including, probably, the Fraser slaves—set out for her new home.

The trip to Orange County took the better part of two days. Travel over the rough roads that were little more than dirt paths was probably tedious for Sarah, yet there were sights along the way to capture her curiosity, too. She had been too young to remember her journey to Fredericksburg as a baby, but she was nearly ten when she came to Orange, perhaps riding in a rough cart or behind a man on a horse or perhaps walking.

The flat grounds of Spotsylvania fell away, and the travelers climbed, almost imperceptibly. The ground slowly rose, and the horizon transformed to rolling hills. Sarah, a town girl, now saw for the first time expanses of virgin forest and her first mountains—a few isolated humps and then the

Sketch of Montpelier as it appeared in the early 1800s. Courtesy James Madison Museum.

southwestern chain, rising in the distance. Ahead lay the town of Orange.

Orange must have seemed pitifully small after Fredericksburg. There was little more to the town, the seat of Orange County, than its rough frame courthouse with its "public lot" holding the clerk's office, jail, and pillory, several taverns, and a few dwellings.

Sarah's new master was one of the wealthiest and most influential planters in the region. At various times Colonel Madison held the positions of vestryman, county militia officer (colonel was his militia rank), and county justice. He was also one of the largest landowners and slaveholders in the county, a successful merchant, and a building contractor. The size and complexity of his operation were something that Sarah soon experienced firsthand. The Madisons' home plantation, Montpelier, was a few miles west of Orange Courthouse, the county seat. Part of the property had been a land grant to Colonel Madison's father in 1723. To this inheritance, Colonel Madison had added other tracts of land. By the time Sarah arrived, he presided over an estate of nearly five thousand acres in central Orange County. Within a few years he acquired additional land in what was then Culpeper (now Madison) County, just north of Orange County.

As a servant to the Madisons, Sarah was apparently trained as a seamstress and laundress (she later made her living at those trades). Sarah probably learned by making clothes for other servants and slaves owned by the Madisons. But since her later customers included wealthy members of the county's prominent families—people who would demand work of a high quality—Sarah must have become quite skilled at her needlework, too skilled to be always relegated to menial sewing tasks. She may well have spent some of her indenture as one of the personal seamstresses of the Madison family.

As a personal servant, in close contact with the Madison family, Sarah would have had other opportunities unlike many other servants and slaves. She could polish her speech, manners, and appearance and make contacts among the Madisons' large network of prominent friends and acquaintances. Sarah demonstrates later, in her career, that she had a quick mind and a sharp business sense, combined with a determination merely not to survive but to achieve a measure of success for herself. No doubt she quickly made the most of the opportunities her new position afforded.

The Montpelier residence that Sarah knew was in its original state, the brick Georgian house completed by Colonel Madison only a few years before he acquired Sarah's indenture, not the stuccoed and columned mansion that Montpelier became in later remodelings. Even before the additions, it was a noteworthy house by local standards. In a time when entire families lived in one- or two-room dwellings, the Montpelier house was the largest and finest in the

SARAH MADDEN

A two-story brick Georgian house built by James Madison, Sr., circa 1760, provided the nucleus of the present Montpelier mansion. Montpelier later became the presidential estate of James Madison, Jr., fourth president of the United States. James was sixteen years old when nine-year-old Sarah Madden joined the household in 1767. She remained there until 1783. Courtesy Montpelier, National Trust for Historic Preservation.

county. Made of solid masonry rather than the common frame construction, Montpelier measured fifty-five by thirty feet. The family lived on the first two floors, and the plainer basement, used for storage and domestic work, was the domain of slaves and servants.

In addition to Colonel Madison, there was his wife, Nelly, and six young Madisons at the time of Sarah's arrival. Two sons had died in infancy, and the surviving children ranged from the sixteen-year-old James, Jr., the future president, to the younger children: Francis, Ambrose, young Nelly, William, and Sarah. Three more children would be born— all to die young—before the birth of the last child, Frances, in 1774. By the start of the Revolution, the family had achieved its final number of the seven offspring who lived to adulthood.

The fact that Sarah's indenture had been owned by the Madison family came as a surprise to me. No family stories ever touched on Sarah's term with the Madisons or even mentioned that she had once been their servant. The few family papers and records relating to Sarah during this time

Nelly Conway Madison, left, wife of James Madison, Sr., right, successful planter, merchant, Virginia gentleman, and father of the fourth president of the United States. Courtesy Belle Grove, Inc.

hint at a tragedy in her life. Perhaps the bitterness and grief resulting from this period in her life were the reason she never spoke of her term of indenture at Montpelier and later at Prospect Hill.

The only surviving family documents concerning Sarah's life during this time are the birth records of her children. Sarah's first baby, Rachel, was born in early 1776, when she was seventeen years old. By the spring of 1782 she had given birth to three children—Rachel, Violet, and David— and was again pregnant. Her daughter Betty was born in August.

Sarah's three oldest children were alive in early 1782. All were living with Sarah on the Montpelier estate, as the 1782 Enumeration of Heads of Households for Orange County,

Virginia, shows eighty-eight Negroes for Colonel James Madison's household in Orange County, as opposed to the eighty-four slaves listed in his personal property taxes in April of the same year. The extra four would be free Negroes: Sarah and her three children.

Sarah's children were also indentured servants to Colonel Madison. The law under which Sarah had been indentured was modified in 1765; calling the practice of binding out the mulatto bastard children of white women until the age of thirty-one "an unreasonable severity towards such children," it provided that thereafter such children would be indentured only until age twenty-one for males and eighteen for females. Nothing, however, was done to shorten the terms of those—Sarah Madden among them—who had been bound out under the old law. The revised law also stated that any child born during an indentured woman's term of servitude was automatically bound to the mother's master. Under the terms of her indenture, Sarah was still bound to serve her master until 1789, when she would be thirty-one years old. The revised law of 1765 grants—for

The shallow waters of the Rapidan River, barely one mile north of Montpelier, was a familiar site to inhabitants of the estate. Courtesy Moss Publications.

Prospect Hill, the home of Francis Madison, where Sarah Madden served the last portion of her indenture. The house is now known as Greenway. Photo, Ann L. Miller. Courtesy Mr. and Mrs. Gilbert K. Queitzsch.

reduced terms—the indentures of Sarah's children to the holder of their mother's indenture, Colonel Madison.

But indentures could be bought, sold, or given away, and sometimes in the early 1780s Colonel Madison gave the indentures of Sarah and her children to his son Francis, who was farming part of his father's land in Culpeper (now Madison) County. Francis was living in Prospect Hill, a plantation on the Rapidan River, some five miles north of Montpelier. Far from being a grand mansion, the Prospect Hill residence was a small frame house containing only four rooms. Francis, married young, already had a number of children to support, and he was chronically short of funds (building and court records show that his house and property were the smallest of any of the Madison brothers). To raise money to support his own children, he decided to sell the indentures of Sarah, Rachel, Violet, David, and Betty.

The buyer was to be a man from Pennsylvania, and Sarah and her children were gathered up to be taken away.

Although her indenture was due to end in six years, she was seized with the fear that once away from the Madisons' property, she and her children would be enslaved.

By law, Sarah's family was protected from enslavement. In Virginia it was perfectly legal to sell a servant's indenture, but there were specific statutes protecting mulatto servants; the same law that revised the terms of servitude downward for mulatto children also stated the penalties for those selling free Negroes or mulattoes as slaves. The penalty for a first offense was a heavy fine, while those convicted of this crime a second time not only were fined but were forced to free the servant and would be themselves sold as servants if they were unable to pay the fine (in 1788 the death penalty was instituted for selling a free Negro or mulatto as a slave in Virginia). By Pennsylvania law, Negroes within that state could only be indentured as servants, not sold as slaves. Yet indenture papers could be lost or destroyed by unscrupulous owners, and Sarah feared, perhaps wisely, that she and her children might be sold into slavery *before* reaching Pennsylvania, with no way to prove that they were free.

It was against the law for a servant to disobey a master, run away, or travel without a pass. But Sarah's fate and the fate of her family might depend on her actions, so she did what few women in her position would have dared to do: She defied her master and escaped. Her destination was Fredericksburg, nearly fifty miles away, and Sarah had no pass. For an escaped servant, merely asking for directions was dangerous, so it took great courage for her to travel alone, especially when all she had to rely on was a distant memory of a trip she had made years before. The trip to Fredericksburg must have taken several agonizing days; she would have had to hide from other travelers, probably by traveling at night and bypassing roads and scampering through fields to avoid being seen, always conscious that her children were in danger.

Once in Fredericksburg, Sarah again did something that few servants would have dared do. Though having committed a criminal act, she bravely made her way to Judge James Mercer, before whom she confessed and pleaded her case. Mercer was the most respected legal mind in Fredericksburg, and perhaps Sarah had heard his name from the Madisons. After her plea, Mercer wrote a letter to Colonel Madison informing him of Sarah's whereabouts and her mission, aiming to help her plight:

Fredericksburg Sepr 25th 1783

Sir—
The Bearer Sarah Madin has been with me to complain that your Son has sold her & the Children to a Man near york town in Pennsylvania the Children she says were collecting to be carried off when she made her escape to ask for protection ag^t. the probable injury she & her children may sustain by her new master's making her & them Slaves— My Acts of Assembly have been so often lent out, that I have now lost that Volume which I think contains an act forbidin[g] masters sending Free Negros or Mulattos out of the State during their Servitude— But whether there is such a Law or not I deem almost immeterial when I address you on this interesting Subject— the Woman can not inform me wether she & her children are sold as Servants or Slaves, and I have no doubts but your Son would not do such a Violence to Rights of Humanity as to sell them otherwise than they are But Sir I know I need not tell a Gent: of your discernment, that the terms of the Sale are very immaterial, when it is so obvious that the purchaser may when he has got these unfortunate People removed from the Evidence of their Rights to freedom, make Slaves of them & sell them as such to persons stil farther off from Justice —the Danger is so probable & the Act of the seller so connected with the Conduct of the purchaser, that he must be in Conscience answerable for the mischief that may follow from the Conduct of the purchaser— therefore I trouble you on this occasion Confiding that you will interpose in this business and prevent the Sale

& thereby arrest the great injustice that may flow from their being sent out of the State— I have not the pleasure of knowing your Son or I should address myself to him, tho' my knowledge of you, woul'd give me far stronger assurances of Success in this Case, than to very many others

I am with real esteem Sir

Y^r. most obed. & very hu[m]ble Servant

J^s Mercer

Perhaps it was late in the evening when Sarah was able to persuade James Mercer to plead her case, or possibly she was exhausted from her journey and he would not let her start back that night. Perhaps as an important jurist he refused to hurry his correspondence. Whatever the reason, it was not until the following day that Judge Mercer folded his letter into an envelope, addressed it to "James Madison, Esquire, Orange," and gave it to Sarah with a pass and allowed her to start back to Montpelier:

Permit the Bearer hereof (Sarah Maden a Mulatto Servant) to pass from this to Mr James Madison's in Orange County allowing her a reasonable time for so doing

Fredericksburg   J^s Mercer
Sept: 26th 1783

Despite all of Sarah's efforts, she was too late. Apparently the sale of their indentures had been speedily completed, and Rachel, age seven, and Violet and David had already been taken away when Sarah returned from her appeal to James Mercer. Had Colonel Madison even then tried to stop the transaction, the lost several days would have made the children's recovery unlikely.* Of Sarah's children, only Betty, just a year old, remained with her mother; we do not know why. Had Sarah managed to hide her baby with some sympathetic slaves or neighbors, or had

---

*No reply from Colonel Madison to James Mercer is known to survive.

On April 6, 1794, Francis Madison prepared and signed this list of Sarah Madden's children. The document was witnessed by William Banks.

she carried the little girl with her all the way to Fredericksburg, to protect her? There is no further mention of Sarah Madden's three oldest children in the family records or local papers.

Francis Madison may in fact have believed that he was helping Sarah and her children by selling their indentures to a Pennsylvanian because Pennsylvania law allowed Negroes to be sold only for terms of indentured servitude, not into slavery. All in all, Pennsylvania's laws were more liberal regarding Negroes than Virginia's. On September 8, 1783—only a few weeks before James Mercer's letter— Francis's oldest brother, James, serving as a member of Congress (which then met in Philadelphia), wrote home to tell his father he had sold his personal slave, Billy, as an indentured servant under Pennsylvania law to avoid bringing him back to slavery in Virginia. Although no reference to Sarah Madden has been found in the surviving papers of the younger James Madison, his sympathy for Billy tells that he would have had similar feelings for Sarah's plight. The future president was aware of the irony of holding Negroes in slavery when Americans had just fought a war to win freedom from Great Britain. He could not, he wrote, bring Billy back to Virginia "merely for coveting that liberty for which we have paid the price of so much blood, and have proclaimed so often to be the right, & worthy the pursuit, of every human being."

The sale of Sarah's and Betty's indentures was canceled, but they were legally still Francis Madison's servants, and they were returned to him to serve the remainder of their indentures. We can only imagine Sarah's feelings about returning to Prospect Hill, where her oldest children had been sold.

When Colonel Madison made out his will in 1787, he confirmed his earlier gift of five slaves and "the servitude of an Indentured Mulatto Woman named Sarah Madden and her Children" to his son Francis. By then Sarah's family included two more children: Polly, born in 1785, and Sarah, born in 1787. One more daughter, Fanny, was born in 1789, just before Sarah's term of servitude ended.

Prospect Hill was Sarah Madden's home for much of the 1780s. The evidence from the 1782 Enumeration of Heads of Households indicates that Sarah was still living in Orange County in 1782. Francis did not have title to the Madison County land until 1784 but was already living on the land earlier; when his father deeded him the property, it was described as the land were Francis "now lives." He was in residence there as early as 1781, as he appears on the first personal property lists for Culpeper County, which were taken in that year. The transfer of Sarah's indenture must have taken place between mid-1782 and the sale of her oldest children's indentures in September 1783. Following her return from her appeal to Judge Mercer, Sarah remained there until the end of her indenture.

As servants Rachel, Violet, and David should have served their indentures of eighteen years (for females) and twenty-one years (for males) and been freed—Rachel in 1794, Violet in 1796, and David in 1802—but we cannot know. Records of Sarah's other children born before the scheduled end of her indenture—Betty and Polly (due to be freed in 1800 and 1803), young Sarah and Fanny (to be freed in 1805 and 1807)—show them living with or near their mother in Culpeper County in the early nineteenth century.

Polly and young Sarah appear in the 1810 Census for Culpeper County. Fanny was married and living in the Shenandoah Valley by the late 1810s, and in a letter written in 1826 she asks about "sister Betty." According to the known birth records of Sarah's grandchildren, all of her daughters' children were born after the time that any indentures would have expired. Perhaps Sarah urged—or even insisted—that her daughters delay marriage or postpone having children until after their indentures ended. Thus the cycle of servitude for the Madden family was broken.

We do not know the whole story of the loss of Sarah's oldest children, but her continued contact with the younger ones portrays her as determined to keep her family together. Sarah probably never learned the final fate of Rachel, Violet, and David. Were they freed after serving their indentures or were they enslaved for life? And what of the younger children born during Sarah's indenture? None of them is mentioned in the inventory of Francis Madison's estate in 1801 although most of them still should have been serving their indentures. Were they freed early, or were their indentures sold to acquaintances of the Madisons in Culpeper County, where Sarah could be found living soon after her own indenture ended in 1789? Or was Sarah so determined to be free herself, see her children free, and have her family together that she bought her children's indentures?

While we do not know the answers, we do know that somehow, surely by great effort on her part, Sarah maintained contact with most of her children. To the end of her life, keeping her family together continued to be Sarah Madden's special concern.

Chapter Three

STEVENSBURG

⨾⧑⨽

Reuben Crump
for washing
March 27 Pieces Since Christmas
*   76 Pieces*
April 108 Pieces

Mr William Banks
to making & mending

March	April
4 Shirts	*2 or 3 Shirts*
3 Crevats	*4 Crevats*
2 pocket Hanker[chiefs]	*3 pr. Stockings*
2 pr Stocking	*1 pr. Breeches*
2 flanl. jaccoats	*1 pr. Draws*
1 towel	*2 Handkerchif*

From Sarah Madden's account books, ca. 1798–1799

Sarah's indenture would have ended in 1789, when she reached thirty-one. No records reveal her whereabouts over the next two years, but by early 1791 she was living in eastern Culpeper County, near the town of Ste-

The sleepy crossroads village of Stevensburg, Virginia, has changed very little since the eighteenth century. It was here that Sarah Madden began a new life after completing her term of servitude. Courtesy Moss Publications.

vensburg, earning her living as a seamstress and laundress. Although the actual date of her arrival in Stevensburg is not recorded, Sarah's account books show that she worked in 1791 for J. C. P. Adams, who lived in the vicinity, and of course, she may have arrived in the area even before then, perhaps right after her indenture ended.* Stevensburg was her home for the rest of her life, and all the names in her account books are people who appear in the Culpeper County records as residents of the Stevensburg area, either in the town itself or within a radius of a few miles.

The counties in the Virginia Piedmont in the late 1700s had few towns; in many counties there was only one town, the county seat. In Culpeper the county seat was the little

---

*Sarah Madden's account books are included in Appendix I as well as excerpted in the following chapter.

town of Fairfax or, as it was known for its major landmark, Culpeper Courthouse. Stevensburg was the second town established in Culpeper County, standing six miles east of the county seat at the crossroads of the Kirtley Road (modern Route 600) and the Carolina Road (Route 633), the major east-west and north-south travel routes. Stevensburg had been founded in 1782 and named for General Edward Stevens, one of Culpeper's revolutionary war heroes. By the time that Sarah would have arrived, around 1790, the town was growing. There was already a Quaker meetinghouse, a merchant's office or two had opened in town, and new houses were being built. Stevensburg had taverns, too, and camping places for the teamsters who hauled produce to and from the trade center for the region, Fredericksburg. Within a few years, Stevensburg was home to more merchants, private schools, a Masonic lodge, and an ammunitions factory. Local businessmen owned plantations outside town, and other large farms stood nearby. By the early nineteenth century the population of Stevensburg rivaled that of the county seat—nearly two hundred people, a sizable town for that place and time.

There were less genteel operations in Stevensburg, too. It had the reputation of being something of a wide-open town, notorious for its horseracing, cockfighting, and gambling. The teamsters' campground near town was known as Wicked Bottom. By the early 1800s Stevensburg's Quakers were gone. They had left, the story goes, to escape the ungodly ways of the town.

By the second decade of the 1800s Stevensburg had begun to decline. Because travelers and traders found it more convenient to use another crossroads east of town for travel between Fredericksburg and the surrounding counties, Stevensburg lost much of its business to the county seat. These crossroads played a central role in the Madden family history.

Sarah Madden, meanwhile, had set herself up in business

in Stevensburg, relying especially on her skill with the needle. Few people in the area owned slave seamstresses. Tax records for late eighteenth and early nineteenth centuries indicate that most slaveholders in Culpeper County owned fewer than five slaves, the majority of these being adult men and children, while many people owned no slaves at all. Skilled seamstresses, slave or free, must have been at a premium. Sarah would have had little difficulty finding customers eager to have her do their sewing and laundry. During her term with the Madisons, Sarah would also have had ample opportunities to meet some of the Madisons' prominent friends and her own potential clients. A number of county and private records show that the Madisons and many of Sarah's Stevensburg customers knew and associated with one another. In time others heard of Sarah by word of mouth or from satisfied customers or from her own efforts. Soon she was doing work for a variety of local people as well as members of well-to-do and influential families like the Bankses, Slaughters, Adamses, and Crumps. Since some of Sarah's customers were large plantation owners and merchants, she was often able to exchange work for needed goods and supplies.

In the days before ready-made clothes or patterns were available, the production of good clothing required a series of highly specialized operations. First, measurements were taken, and then a pattern was made. Next, the cloth was cut properly—not just to pattern size but to ensure that the cloth would not shrink or stretch out of shape. The pieces were then sewn together by hand, with stitching small and fine enough to suit a fashionable lady or gentleman yet durable enough to last for years, for good clothes were often handed down through several generations, remade for each new owner. Sarah had to fit and make her own patterns for each individual client and sew each stitch by hand. She must have been a skilled seamstress to make such well-fitting clothes.

Washing clothes involved boiling them in a kettle over an open fire, followed by a strenuous scrubbing to get them clean. Then came the drying, pressing, and ironing—that is, hanging some clothes on a line or over bushes until they dried, stretching others on frames so they dried evenly without shrinking, and then ironing them with a heavy metal iron that had to be reheated every minute or so on a metal plate over a fire (few people then had stoves). Between her household and business work, Sarah's days must have started before dawn and ended long after dark, by the light of a homemade candle, crude oil lamp, or firelight.

Sarah's account books for those early years in Culpeper were kept for her by one of her employers, William Banks, who combined the trades of merchant and insurance agent. Because he was special agent for the Mutual Assurance fire insurance company, his signature appears on most Culpeper County policies of that era. Several of her account books for the late 1790s have survived among the family papers. The books are simple and handmade; the sheets of rough paper were carefully folded and stitched together, perhaps by Sarah herself, into booklets no bigger than the palm of a hand. Inside, the pages are covered with entries. Sarah's account books show that she made, mended, and laundered dozens—sometimes hundreds—of items of clothing each month for her clients.

[First account book, ca. 1797–1798]

Reuben Crump for washing		John Crump
June 25	To washing a dozen [illegible]	To washing 10 Dozen /2
	To making 3 Shirts	To mending 7 p^r Stocking @ 4d.
	mending 1 jaccoat [jacket] 1/6	To D^o 1/pr Breaches 9d.
25	mending 6 p^r Stockings 4d. 2/	Wm Banks Acct. with Sarah Madden
June 28	to washing 5 pieces	1797

July   5   D° to 8 pieces
      10   D° to 6 D°   )
      20   D° to 6 D°   )
      27   To 3 Pieces)
              Drawd of
Agˢ 6
      19   To 14 Pieces)
Sept   4 Pieces
         12 Pieces
Oct   15 Pieces
         10 Pieces
         14 Ditto
         11 Pieces
         16 Pieces
         11   "
Janry   7 After Christmas
            (Reuben Crump,
            junʳ)
March   27 Pieces Since
            Christmas
         76 Pieces
Apr   108 Pieces

Dʳ William Banks to washing
From 1st Day of January

24th Day of June to washing
16 Dozen 8 1/2 at 4/6 pʳ Dozen
June 28 To Washing 8 Pices
July   5 D° to 26 pieces
      10 D° to 10 D°
   20 D° to 29 D°
   27 D° to 22 Pieces
Agst   6   )
      15   )To 23 Pieces
Aug.   22 Pieces
           40 Pieces
           29 Pieces
           23 Pieces

To Makeing 2 winter suits for
James
To D° 2 flanel jaccoats [jack-
ets]
To D° 2 pʳ flanel Draises
[dresses]
To D° 4 pʳ Linen Brice James
To D° 4 Shirts   D°
1796
To D° 2 Shirts for James
      D° 1 Coat
      D° 1 [illegible]
1797
      D° 2 pʳ Linen Breachings
      D° 2 Shirts
96
      D° 2 Suits for James P
      Alcock
To making 1 pʳ Sheets
   "   2 piller [pillow] Cases
   "   2 flanil jaccoats

Mr. William Banks washing Acᵗ
To making 1 Coat & 1 Pair
Breachs for James
2 Brown Linen Shirts
Sam. 2 Shirts
1 Pair of Sheets for Reubin
1 pʳ Draws
3 pʳ Breaches
2 Shirts for Sam
2 pʳ Breaches

Oct.   18 Pieces
            61 Pieces
            23 Pieces

1798

            26 Pieces Since Chr.
            56 Pieces Since Chr.
            153 Pieces
            159
            36 Pieces Drawn of

For just one of her customers, Reuben Crump, she made three shirts, mended a jacket and six pairs of stockings, and washed seventeen items of clothing in a single week in June 1797. In the first four months of 1798 she washed 218 pieces for the Crump family alone, including 108 pieces in one month. This busy time was in the winter and early spring, so Sarah had to haul water and wash these clothes outside during the coldest months of the year.

The accounts for the family of William Banks show that Sarah made coats, winter suits, flannel jackets and dresses, shirts, breeches, sheets, and pillowcases for them. This was in addition to laundry work. In 1797, for instance, she washed 326 items of clothing for the Bankses, and in 1798, 430. In return, she received sewing supplies, items of food, and household goods from the Banks store; her accounts for mid-1796 record her getting brown sugar, a meal sifter, a quart of whiskey (the small amount suggests that it was probably used as a medicine), coffee, shoes, molasses, salt, and a bushel of corn. The next year's list includes coffee, brown and white sugar, needles, thread, a thimble, nineteen yards of brown linen, another quart of whiskey, a knife, and "rappins" (wrappings).

	C^r	
To 1 Coffee at 2/3	2	3
1 1/2 Brown Sugar	1	6

12 yds Brown Linon @ 1/6	18	0
7 yd D° at 1/3	8	9
1 Knife @ 1/6	1	6
Brown thread 6		6
1 Dozen needles 6		6
Rappins 4/	4	0
1 Thimble 3		3
1/2 Sugar 1/6	[illegible]	

£ 21 3

[Pounds, shillings, pence]

1 yd Thread 1/3	1	6
1 quart wiskey 1/6	1	3
1 Sugar 1/3	1	6

25 1

Sary Madden

1792	D^r To Slaughter & Banks	
Novr 8	8 yards Stuff @ 1/6	0. 12. 0.
1793	3 ditto Linin @ 1/6	0. 3. 0.
April 12	1 7/8 dito ditto @ 1/6	0. 1. 8/4
	1 ditto ditto	0. 1. 0 1/2
	5 ditto ditto	0. 5. 0.

C^r

By Cash at difr tim[e]s   3. 4 1/2

£ 0.19.4 1/4

[Pounds, shillings, pence]

By 2 Busls. Corn @ 4/8   4. 8

Errs Extd P R. Thom

Sarah Madden Acc^t wth
William Banks & C°
Dr Sarah Maddin   In account with William Banks & C°   C^r
1796

June 19 To	4 cu brown Sugar 4s.1 meal sifter 2/9 P self	6 9	
26	1 quart Whiskey pd.	2 –	
27	2 cu Coffee 4/6 1 pair shoes 6/9 P self	11 3	
	1 gallon Molasses	5	6 16 9

July	3	1 peck Salt P Sam		1	8
	11	1 Bushel Corn rec^d of Mr. Slaughter		5	–
			£	1 12	2

[Pounds, shillings, pence]

The few items on Sarah's store accounts tell a familiar story for that era: Manufacturing in America was only beginning, and little in the way of ready-made goods was available. Even if such goods were available, few people had large amounts of money on hand to purchase them. Cash money was in short supply, and bartering was a major part of the economy. People had to be self-sufficient especially in rural areas. Sarah Madden, like many others, raised or made almost everything that she and her children needed. The only things she bought were supplies for her business and staples that she could not grow or make herself.

Sarah's account books carefully list the number and kind of items she washed or sewed—although separate prices are seldom given—indicating that she charged according to the number of pieces. The 1799 account of one of her customers, James Dicerson, shows that her rates for washing were three shillings for every dozen items.

Mr James Dicerson   D^r to washing
  At 3/Dozen
Jan
6 Shirts
2 p^r Stockings
Febr
2 p^r Breaches
3 Handkerchiefs
2 Shirts
15 Pieces @ 3/p^r D.   3.9
Mar
3 Shirts
3 jaccoats

34

1 Handkerchief
Apr 2 week
3 Shirts
3 Shirts
4 Shirts
1 p^r Stocking
2 p^r Breechs
2 jaccoats
22 Pieces at 3 p^r D^o 6.0
Mending 2/8

In contrast, the costs of the items she received from William Banks's store were always recorded, showing that she was trading some work for supplies. The three shillings Sarah received for every dozen items she washed equaled, for example, the cost of two yards of linen or half the cost of a pair of shoes.

The income and supplies were going toward the support of Sarah's ever-increasing family. Wherever her older children were at this time, others were coming now: Nelly was born in 1793, and Nancy in 1796, and at least two more followed. The birth records in the Madden family documents list a total of eleven children born to Sarah Madden. Indeed, there may have been even more; Culpeper County records and Madden family papers for the early nineteenth century mention a William Madden and a Samuel Madden, both of an age to be Sarah's sons, although they are not listed in the family birth records.

According to census records, Sarah Madden was always the head of her household. If there was a man she considered her husband, he must have lived elsewhere. Sarah remained a Madden throughout her life; no record has been found naming the father of any of her children. Since she lived in several places during the time her children were born, there may have been different men in her life over the years. Slaves could not legally marry, and even free Negroes and mulattoes often found it almost impossible to get married in legally recognized ceremonies, as the marriage laws of Virginia were not held to apply to free Negroes. Legally the marriages of all free Negroes were considered common-law relationships, and because of this, many white licensed ministers were not willing to perform marriage ceremonies for Negroes. Most Negroes, slave or free, married by "jumping the broomstick"—that is, having their own ceremonies or agreements, whether casual or elaborate.

With more mouths to feed and growing children, Sarah needed her wealthier clients more than ever, because of the money and goods they could provide at present and because in the future they could provide references and more jobs, for her and for her children. Sarah needed only to keep their trust and goodwill.

Sarah was caught between two worlds. She was more than a slave, less than a white woman. Her skills and free status gave her some chance at acceptance in a white world, but there was a price to pay for this. She depended on whites for her livelihood, in a time when and place where many whites considered free Negroes immoral, dangerous, and potential subversives. Sarah's life-style had to be quiet; she had to avoid the company of slaves and even that of many free Negroes, so she wouldn't be suspected of involvement in crimes or slave rebellions.

There was another consideration for Sarah: If she could not support her children, they would be taken away from her and bound out, as she herself had once been. Sarah realized that she needed the employment of the white community, but set hard in her soul was the knowledge that if

Rachal Madden. Daughter of Sarah Madden, was Born March the 10.th 1776 –

Violett Madden, Daughter of Sarah Madden, was Born June the 12.th 1778.

David Madden. Son of Sarah Madden was Born April the 21.st 1780.

Betty Madden Daughter of Sarah Madden, was Born August the 26.th 1782.

Polly Madden. Daughter of Sarah Madden, was Born March the 2.d 1785. –

Sarah Madden. Daughter of Sarah Madden was Born May the 2.d 1787.

Fanny Madden. Daughter of Sarah Madden was Born July the 6.th 1789.

Nelly Madden. Daughter of Sarah Madden, was Born September the 19.th 1793

Nancy Madden. Daughter of Sarah Madden was Born monday night the 25.th of April 1796

Willis Madden Son of Sarah Madden was Born June the 1799. –

This document listing Sarah's children was written between 1799 and 1802. The author of the document is unknown.

37

she was going to make a future for herself and for her children, there was only one person whom she could truly count on—and that was herself.

Family stories describe Sarah Madden as an independent, resourceful woman, and she must have been, to survive on her own, keep her family together, and finally gain a measure of relative prosperity. By the late 1790s she had begun to have something to show for her hard work. Her sewing and laundry business was good and growing. She was also developing another business. Her accounts with J. C. P. Adams in 1791–1792 mention a cow and calf, for which she paid or traded nearly a year's wages. It was an expense, but also an investment. The cow gave milk and would produce another calf every year. The male calves could be eaten or sold, while the heifers could be kept to produce milk and calves in their turn. By the end of the 1790s Sarah's cow herd was increasing. She bought or traded work for some, and others were heifers that she had raised. She sold the butter she made from the milk and also had enough calves so that she could sell some every year. More money was coming in, and life was beginning to get better for Sarah's family.

Sarah satisfied her children's physical needs, giving them food, clothing, and shelter, and she gave them much more. She gave them love, a sense of self-respect, and purpose. She had come from nothing, had built herself up through her own determination and effort, and, most important, had kept her family together, against the odds. Sarah was a living example to her children of hard work, determination, concern for her family, and pride: pride in one's self, in one's work, and in the fact that they were *free*—not freed—Negroes, because the Maddens had never been owned. And this especially has remained a source of pride in the Madden family through the generations. Sarah's children had her blood and her will to survive. She wanted them to remember these things always and hold their heads up.

With the close of the eighteenth century a son was born to Sarah Madden in 1799. More than any other of Sarah's children, he was to take his mother's example to heart. He was my great-grandfather Willis Madden.

Chapter Four

WILLIS MADDEN

〜❧〜

To the General Assembly of Virginia

. . . It must be known to many of your body, that the Mechanick trades and arts are fast falling into the hands of the black population. Your memorialists venture to assert that the time is near at hand, without your interposition, when the most common and useful trades will be professed and carried on by slaves, within the knowledge of your memorialists the blacksmith's trade is at present allmost exclusively carried on by slaves, that the trades of stone mason, plaisterer, painter, bricklayer, miller, carpenter and cooper and not uncommon the trades of tanner, carrier, shoe and boot maker, distiller, and the fine handicrafts of all kinds are executed by slaves, the effect of which is to throw out of employ the white mechanick, and to degrade his profession, depressing at the time his labor below its fair value and to cause him to be improverished, and finally drive him from his home and native state to find in the west an assylum where he will be appreciated according to his honesty, industry and ingenuity. . . . We your memorialists pray your honorable body to pass a law for the encouragement and protection of the white mechanick, by Prohibiting any slave, free negro or mulatto, being placed as an apprentice in any manner whatsoever to learn [a] trade or art, under severe and onorous penalties upon the owner of such slave or servant, as well as upon the white person who may undertake to teach such

slave, free negro, or mulatto his art or trade. And your memorialists as in duty bound will ever pray &c &c.

> *Culpeper County Legislative Petition, December 9, 1831 (signed by 113 Culpeper County citizens)*

As is the case with Sarah's other children, there is no documentation of the father of Willis Madden. Madden family legends, in fact or fancy, describe him as "George Washington's coachman," although Washington's journals place Washington—and, probably, his coachman—at Mount Vernon all through the summer and early fall of 1798, when Sarah would have become pregnant. This legend could instead be referring to the more realistic possibility that Willis or one of Sarah's other children might have been fathered by a slave or former slave of President James Madison.

Sarah Madden was forty-one when Willis was born, already an older woman for those days. Within the next decade her skill in needlework deteriorated as her hands began to stiffen with age. She didn't need nimble fingers to wash clothes or churn butter, though, and her laundry and dairy businesses gradually became her main sources of work.

As Sarah became older, she began to depend on her children more and more. Willis Madden went to work early to help support his mother and his sisters still at home. He started out doing odd jobs, like farm work, in the neighborhood, but he followed Sarah's example and was always watching for new opportunities. He had the same natural intelligence and instinct for survival as his mother, a capacity to see what had to be done and then do it, taking matters into his own hands and rising to his responsibilities. By the time he was in his teens, he was handling most of the family's business for his aging mother, and the family began to think of him as the new head of the household.

Like most other free Negroes, the Maddens rented the place where they lived. The family's exact whereabouts

Willis Madden's "free papers," dated September 19, 1826. Free Virginia Negroes were required to carry this document on their persons at all times for identification.

during Sarah's early years in Stevensburg are uncertain, but by the 1810s, perhaps even earlier, they were living east of town, in an area that had become home to several families of free Negroes, among them the Hackleys, Clarks, Bannisters, and Bundys.

The Hackleys were apparently some of the former slaves

of John Hackley, a merchant of Stevensburg who died in 1801 and made arrangements in his will to free his slaves. The Clarks were headed by William Clark, a mulatto who had served in the revolutionary war. He was old and poverty-stricken. His hands were almost too stiff to close around a hoe, and he was barely able to do the farm work that was his only livelihood. He and his wife and children made do with odd jobs and, later, with the small pension that he got for his revolutionary army service.*

Others living nearby were the Bannister family and the Bundys. Oliver Bannister, like Sarah, had come to the Stevensburg area from Orange County, and also like Sarah, was a mulatto who had formerly been an indentured servant. The Bundys were tall, dark-skinned, and Indian- or Asian-looking, with slanted eyes and straight hair. They claimed to have come from the island of Madagascar, off Africa (they still looked the same and still claimed to be from Madagascar a century later, when as a child I knew the Bundy family).

It was in this community that Willis Madden reached manhood. By the early 1820s, and probably earlier—the exact date is not known to us—Sarah and her family had moved to the old Barnes place. John Barnes had died in 1799, leaving a wife and children. The family couldn't keep up the small farm. The buildings were in need of repair, and the land—never good—was in poor shape from neglect. The Barnes family had moved away and rented out the small farm. Soon Sarah and some of her children moved in as tenants.

Sarah is shown as head of her household in the 1810 Census listing but does not appear on the Culpeper County personal property tax rolls until 1816, so it was probably around this time that she moved to the Barnes farm. Prior to this, she probably lived on one of the local plantations and was

---

*William Clark's revolutionary pension papers are in Appendix II.

not recorded in the tax records, although family records show that she owned taxable goods—her cows—before that date.

There was nothing notable about the old Barnes farm itself, but it stood at a well-traveled crossroads, the same crossroads that had funneled most of the traffic away from Stevensburg and now handled most of the area's Fredericksburg-bound trade. Next to the Barnes farm stood the old Great Fork Church, the oldest church in the county, nearly a hundred years old. Built in 1732, it was the main parish church during the colonial period. But the colonial era was long past, and after the Revolution, the Anglican Church, reorganized as the Episcopal Church, was no longer the official or "established" church, but a reminder of the British government. The church had fallen on hard times: It was no longer supported by taxes, and its property had been confiscated by the state government. By the time the Maddens came to the Barnes property, the Great Fork Church was in poor shape. The building badly needed repair, and services were seldom held there anymore.

The only new thing at the Great Fork Church was Joseph Downman's tomb. A merchant from Lancaster County in eastern Virginia, Downman had died in 1799—only a few months after Willis was born—while on a business trip to the Shenandoah Valley. He was a relative of the Hamiltons, who lived near Stevensburg, and they arranged for him to be buried at the old church. Downman had an elaborate tomb, brick sides rising off the ground and a flat stone slab covering him, inscribed: "Here lies the body of Joseph Downman, Esq., of Lancaster County, who died . . . the 24th of September 1799, leaving a wife, three sons, and seven daughters."

Willis Madden knew Joseph Downman only as a pile of rock and bricks in the pasture beside the crumbling church, not as a once-living person. But he was getting a close look at the mortality of another person, someone whom he knew well and who was very real to him. In 1818 Sarah Madden turned sixty. The family papers for this time contain no more sewing and laundry accounts. Sarah's ability to do fine needlework had probably stopped altogether, and it is unlikely that she could still do the heavy work involved in washing and ironing large amounts of clothes. But her papers show that she still owned a small herd of cows and made a living selling the butter and the calves. Besides her small dairy business, Sarah's interests in old age revolved around her family and the church.

The Maddens were devout Baptists, making regular journeys to the Mount Pony Baptist Meetinghouse eight miles west of the old Barnes farm, on a hill still known as Mount Pony, near the county seat. At this time many Negroes attended church with whites. Later they were forbidden to have separate congregations and ministers unless whites were in attendance. The family probably walked to many church meetings or sometimes rode with neighbors when they could. Later, toward the end of her life, Sarah acquired an old horse, and perhaps a cart as well, when the long walks became too difficult for her.

The family Sarah had strived to keep together was scattering. By the time of the census in 1810, Sarah had only the youngest children at home with her. Young Sarah and Polly already had several children of their own and had their own households in the neighborhood. Sarah, listed in the census as "Sarah Madden, Sr.," was the head of a household of five free Negroes (ages and sex not given, but most likely herself and her four youngest children). By the next census, in 1820, her household, all described as "Free Colored," contained two boys and two girls under the age of fourteen, apparently grandchildren; one male under twenty-six, Willis; two females under age twenty-six, probably daughters; and one woman over forty-five, Sarah herself.

The other girls were soon leaving home as well. Fanny married one of the Hackleys and went to live in the Shenandoah Valley. Nelly soon joined them, and letters from Fanny to the Culpeper Maddens mention that Nelly was living with Fanny's family by 1819. Nancy was there also by the mid-1820s, although she later returned to Culpeper County and appears on the 1830 Census there.

1810 Census, Culpeper County (p. 27)

Polly Madden	4 Free Negroes in Household
Sarah Madden, Jr.	3 Free Negroes in Household
Sarah Madden, Sr.	5 Free Negroes in Household

1820 Census, Culpeper County (p. 87)

Polly Madden	1 Free Colored Male under 14
	3 Free Colored Females under 14
	1 Free Colored Female under 45
Sally Madden	4 Free Colored Males under 14
	3 Free Colored Females under 14
	1 Free Colored Female under 45
Sarah Madden	2 Free Colored Males under 14
	1 Free Colored Male under 26
	2 Free Colored Females under 14
	2 Free Colored Females under 26
	1 Free Colored Female over 45

1830 Census, Culpeper County
[p. 89]

Nancy Madden	1 Free Colored Male under 10
	1 Free Colored Male between 10 and 24
	1 Free Colored Female under 10
	2 Free Colored Females between 10 and 24
	1 Free Colored Female between 24 and 36

[p. 151]

Samuel Madden	2 Free Colored Males under 10
	1 Free Colored Male between 36 and 55
	1 Free Colored Female between 24 and 36

There were still visits among the families, but now with miles and mountains between Sarah and several of her children, the visits were less frequent, if perhaps even more cherished. On occasion the various Madden families met at the Mount Pony church, for a reunion as well as worship. By 1819 Fanny's son John William Hackley had learned to read and write and was keeping Sarah informed of the family's whereabouts. His letters were probably read to Sarah and her family by a sympathetic neighbor.

[To] Sarah Matten
Stevensburg Culpeper County Virginia

April 11 1819 dear gran mother I have embraced the oppertunity to inform you that I am well father and mother also and I hope these few lines will find you the same and all the rest of your family[.] mother did expect to have the pleasure of being with you this day she got disappointed fathers horses was all very sick with the distemper [page torn] . . . could not come [.] you may expect mother and aunt nelly and my self the first week in may if mother and aunt nelly and myself if we dont come the first week in may tell all my aunt and uncle willis to meet us at mount pony the second Sunday in may if we are alive and have our healt[h] we will be there to meeting[.] father and mother desires to be remembered to you uncle james and his family is well ma desires to be remembered to you all
dear Granmother you must excuse my letter being I am a new hand I have nothing more at present to write you I remain your dear affectionate granson

John William Hackley   my hand and seal

John William, having just learned to write, considered himself "a new hand" at the business of letter writing. His father, Fanny's husband, was probably William Hackley, a free Negro who appears in the Rockingham County Census of 1820 and 1830. Another free Negro, James Hackley, lived nearby. He was probably William's brother and apparently was the "uncle James" mentioned in John William's letter.

It would have been very hard for Sarah to live alone; she was increasingly feeble and sometimes too sick to care for herself. Although the other children were moving away, Willis knew that he had to wait. Sarah depended on him, and he felt a great responsibility toward her. He would take care of old Sarah as long as she lived.

Sarah must have been proud of Willis. He had worked on the local farms since he was a boy, and like many other free Negroes then, he might well have spent his whole life as a laborer or small craftsman. But Willis was different; energetic and ambitious, he wanted more out of life. He was constantly trying to learn new things, to develop new skills. Family documents and legends mention Willis Madden's many talents and abilities. He learned shoemaking and became an excellent cobbler, with customers from among the most prominent families of the area. In addition, he became a blacksmith and did ironwork and made and sold nails. He built a still, sold the brandy and whiskey he made, and soon was supplying the neighborhood. When he had saved a little money, he bought a horse and an old wagon and set himself up as a teamster, hauling goods back and forth between different points in Culpeper County and Fredericksburg.

In the early 1820s Willis Madden got married. His bride was Kitty Clark, daughter of old William Clark, the revolutionary war veteran. Kitty was a small woman, a "bright mulatto"—quite light-skinned. Their marriage is not recorded: Willis and Kitty "jumped the broomstick" without an "official" wedding, as was the custom. But if the local authorities didn't consider the marriage legal, Willis and Kitty did. It was the start of a lifetime commitment, and it was apparent that Willis and Kitty were together to stay. People began to refer to Kitty not as Kitty Clark but as Kitty Madden.

In 1823 the Madden family passed through a crisis. Mariah Madden, old Sarah's youngest daughter, had a child. The father was Christopher Bannister, but they were not living in the same household. Mariah had several other children by this time. The county authorities determined that Mariah could not support her children by herself and began proceedings to take the children away and bind them out. There was also the threat that the households of other Maddens might be investigated to see if there were similar cases.

All of Sarah's worst fears might now come true. After a lifetime of working to keep her family together, she was faced, in her sixty-fifth year, with the possibility of seeing her labor and dreams crumble. Most of her daughters in Culpeper County lived alone. None was legally married or had a husband on the premises. Many Negro women were heads of their households than, and since Negroes' marriages were not considered legal, relations between men and women were sometimes casual. Some free Negroes, such as Willis Madden and Kitty Clark, or Fanny Madden Hackley, had secure, long-term relationships. Others, such as old Sarah and her daughters Sarah, Polly, and Mariah, had husbands living elsewhere or perhaps a series of marriages or less permanent relationships with a succession of different men through their lives. Under investigation by the county authorities, most of Sarah's daughters would have a hard time proving they could take care of their children. But in fact, their families were being supported—by Willis.

As in the days of Mary Madden, only children whose families or fathers could guarantee their support were safe from the threat of indenture. Willis had always set aside a large part of his earnings to help support his mother and sisters. He continued to be the main support of the family, and in this case he needed character references and affidavits from whites to prove his claims.

Willis Madden was careful in his associations and his business dealings. He had built upon the contacts and influential customers that Sarah had cultivated and had learned his mother's lessons. The family legends tell that like her, he was quiet and polite, but never servile. Some members of the white community considered that he "knew his place." They could think what they wanted, and it would be true: Willis Madden did know where his place was—at the head of his family and his business.

He conducted himself with a sense of quiet dignity and competence. To some extent, Willis would always be classed by his color: a free Negro, subject to the restrictions of law. But in many of his daily dealings, this color barrier was minimized. If the county authorities did not yet know Willis Madden's reputation, the people around Stevensburg did. As with his mother, Willis's skills, dignity, support of his family, and honesty had already led many of the local people to accept him—to a far greater extent than was usually given a free Negro—simply as he wanted to be accepted: as another human being, as a man.

Yet he still needed the references of whites to prove his case. Willis Madden couldn't waste time on questions of fairness or unfairness; he set out to get what he needed. He began to spread the word about the threat that faced his family, and his pain must have been evident as he approached past and present neighbors and employers.

Through the good name that his mother had established and through his own reputation, Willis Madden was able to produce a number of references. Albert G. Berry, who owned the nearby Peola (sometimes spelled Paoli) Mills, and several other wealthy landowners—William S. Jones, George Wallis, John Henshaw, and Henry Field—all testified to the honesty and character of Willis Madden and his family:

WILLIS MADDEN

I Do hereby Certify that I have known Willis Mattin fir a long time and have hired him several times and was always Pleas[ed] with his work and he also passed through the plantation and the family of them also, and I never miss^d any thing after them at all During 8 years and was Supposed to be Honest By all that Ever I Chatted with about them and Heard that Willis Mattins Leighbor went to the support of his mother & his Sisters and also heard that Sams work was to support Nancy and Her children which he told me Him self sam did and as for their suffering for any thing I Dont known why they should when old Sarah Matten sells from 5 lbs. to 6 lbs. of butter per week. Giveing under my hand this 11th Day of June 1823.

William S. Jones

I do hereby Certify that I have Known Willis Madden for a long time and have hired him frequently and was always pleased with his work and I never herd anything dishonest of him but always understood by hs neighbors that he was thought to be honest and industerous
giving under my hand this the 11 june 1823

George Wallis

I have known Willis Madden four years, he had done a good deal of work for me since my acquaintance with him. I have also had dealings with him and believe him to be both honest and industrious

John Henshaw

I have known Willis Maden Several years he behaves well is Honest so far as I Know or Hear

Henry Field

I have known Willis Maden several years and he behaves well and I believe him to be honest and industrious. I also believe that he bought a good deel of corn this year I know of his buying some of Mrs Shepherd which he had ground at our Mill and some of Mr Calhoun I also know him to be a

51

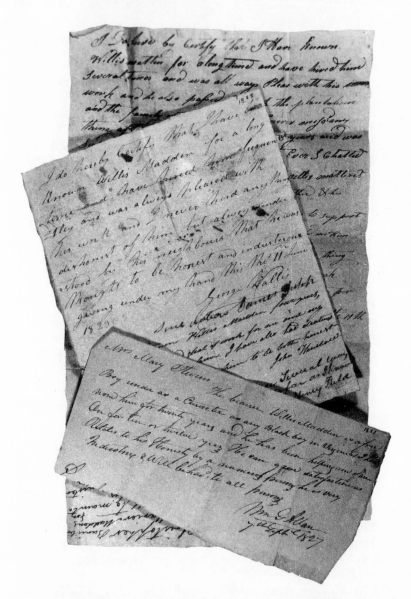

On September 7, 1827, William Allen wrote an endorsement of Willis Madden attesting to Willis's honesty, adding that Willis was "very industrious and well behaved to all persons." Other endorsements bear the signatures of equally prominent individuals of the locale: George Wallis, William Jones, and Henry Field.

An exhibit of frugality not uncommon in that era, the bottom of William Jones's endorsement of Willis Madden contains yet another legal document: Christopher Bannister's acknowledgment of paternity for Sally Madden. Signed and witnessed by Albert Berry, the writer agrees to bind himself "to maintain said child lawfully."

verry good shoemaker as he has made several pare of shoes for me.

> Albert G. Berry
> Paoli June 11th 1823

These, along with an affidavit from the child's father, Christopher Bannister, that he would help support his child, settled the matter.

> This is to certify that I Christopher Banist[er] the acknowledged father of Marier Maddens child Sally do hereby bind myself to maintain said Child lawfully.
> Test   Albert G. Berry   his
>   Christopher X Baniste
>   cross   June 11, 1823

County Justice George Lightfoot rendered his decision in a standard note to Thomas Humphries, an overseer of the poor, on June 12, 1823:

> From the general character given of the Madin family, stating, that they have good names, as to honesty, I think it would be improper to rob them of their Children by binding them out, it is still necessary to charge them to be careful in having any intercourse with slaves & not to deal with them, otherwise they would & ought to forfeit the good opinion which the people are disposed to entertain of them.

The proceedings were dropped, and Sarah could rest without the fear that had been haunting her. The case, which came under the jurisdiction of the overseers of the poor, is not recorded in the Culpeper County court records. The only surviving evidence of this near tragedy to the family is the collection of letters and affidavits found among the Madden family papers.

This was the last storm that Sarah Madden had to weather. She closed her eyes forever a few months later, in early 1824. The family chose a peaceful grove on the farm for her gravesite, and they buried Sarah Madden under the oaks. She had been like an oak herself, her roots—her beginnings—stained with the dark soil of poverty and fear, but from these roots had come strong growth, solid at the heart, with many branches: her descendants.

Fifty years earlier Sarah's mother Mary Madden, had gone to a pauper's grave, but Sarah would not have such a lonely or hurried funeral. With Sarah's close family, her burial must have been filled with love and mourning, with as many family members present as could attend, from her older daughters, already in middle age, to her tiny great-grandchildren hardly steady on their feet.

Although no mention of old Sarah's funeral survives in family documents, the death of young Sarah Madden two years later prompted a letter to Willis from his sister Fanny Hackley asking when the funeral was to be and inquiring about the orphaned children. Fanny's letter illustrates that the family was very close at this time and that Madden funerals were times for the family to gather.

Few people then could afford carved tombstones, and the Maddens were not among them, but Sarah's children had settled on an even more impressive monument. Old Sarah was buried by a huge boulder which stood in the middle of the oak grove. It would never wear and would never fall— a fitting monument to a remarkable woman.

Both family papers and legends preserve the story of the site of Sarah Madden's burial. Sarah was renting the Barnes place when she died—the administration papers for her estate include rent payments—and like most people in those days, she would have been buried near her home. Willis Madden always referred to the boulder as marking the "old family cemetery" to his grandson T. O. Madden, Sr., my father, indicating that she was buried there. The area around the boulder remained a family burial ground for five generations of Maddens; the last burial there, in 1935, was of one of Sarah Madden's great-great-great-grandchildren, a thir-teen-year-old daughter of Odenla Madden Phillips, daugh-ter of T. O. Madden, Sr.

Willis was made administrator of Sarah's estate. She left no will. Her estate was not even mentioned in the county records, and the only record is among the family papers. An inventory was made of her livestock, enumerating her sources of livelihood: a red and white cow and calf, an old red cow, a short-tail cow and calf, a dark red heifer, "One dark red cow buf." (a "buffalo" or hornless cow), four more calves, and "One old black horse." The total valuation was $71.50, equivalent to nearly a year's income for many fam-ilies then.

We the undersigned valued twelve head of cattle belonging to the Estate of Sarah Maddon deceased on the valuation below—

October 7th	One red & white cow & calf	$12.00
	One old red cow	7.00
	One white face cow	9.00
	One short tail cow & calf	10.00
	One dark red heifer	10.00
	One dark red cow buf.	
	[i.e., buffalo or hornless]	10.00
	Three calf 2.50 each	7.50
	One yearling calf	3.00
	One old black horse	3.00
		$71.50

Armistead Gordon
James A. Gordon
James Turner

The accounting of her estate covers the period from 1821 to 1822 as well as 1824 and 1825. The earlier accounts may refer to her debts or her various illnesses at times for several years before her death. There are no accounts for 1823. William S. Jones's affidavit in 1823 that "old Sarah Matten sells from 5 lbs. to 6 lbs. of butter per week" is proof that she was still alive and fairly healthy then. The last two years of accountings support the family legend, which gives her death date as early in 1824, so these records for 1824–1825 must represent the final administration of her estate, after her death.

Estate of Sarah Maddon

	To Willis Maddon	D^r	
1821	to one pen of Shucks & hauling	$5.00	
	paid Colo. Long for pasturage	6.00	
	paid Jacob Stout this sum	6.00	
1822	paid John S. Wallace for fodder	3.00	
	paid Mrs Shakelford for waggon hire	1.00	
	paid John Hinshaw for straw	3.00	
	paid Thomas Kelly for waggon hire	1.00	
	paid Henry Abbott for waggon hire	.66	⅔
1824	paid John Bailey on acct of Daniel Cole	1.00	
	paid John Hinshaw	.50	
	paid Henry Abbott for waggon hire	.66	⅔
	D° D° D°	.50	
	paid Sarah Abbott for daughter Lucy hire	1.50	
1825	paid John Bailey	.45	
		29.78	⅓
	to Mr Barnes for Rent	24.00	
	to Mr D. Cole	3.00	
	to Mr Nall	4.30	
	to Mr Gordon	3.50	
	to Nancy Madden	5.00	
		$69.58	⅓

From Sarah's estate came payments for pasturage, for straw and fodder, for wagon hire, and for money to pay Sarah Abbott "for daughter Lucy hire," the last possibly for housekeeping or farm help for the ailing Sarah Madden. Also included were rent payments to one of the Barnes family.

Some of Sarah's livestock went to pay bills; the rest, and Sarah's personal belongings, were divided among her children. But there was one thing that Willis kept for himself, either by legacy or design: his mother's collection of documents. Sarah had never learned to read or write, but she had kept every document or scrap of paper pertaining to the family. These were the only tangible evidence of who she was and what her life had been. The copy of her indenture paper from the Madison family was there, as well as the papers giving the birth dates of her children and grandchildren, family letters, her old account books, and, last the documents of support for the Maddens Willis had gathered that had saved her family and enabled her to die in peace. To these, Willis added the administration account and appraisal of her estate. But Willis also looked to the future. The record of the family had to be maintained and preserved. When Willis and his family moved to new quarters, he packed up the papers and took them with him.

The several years after old Sarah's death were times of change for Willis and Kitty in their family and household. Willis's sister young Sarah died in 1826, and Willis and other family members helped find homes for her children. Even though Willis could not read or write, someone in the neighborhood was able to write and read letters for him. In this fashion the members of the family who had moved away were told of Sarah's death. Fanny, styling herself formally as Frances Hackley, wrote Willis from Rockingham County offering to help find homes for the children. Fanny was a very religious woman. She inquired about family members, worried about her dead sister's spiritual state, and asked when the funeral would be preached (funerals were often held weeks or months after burial in those days, either in church or whenever a minister could visit the gravesite). She also invited Willis and Kitty to the upcoming August camp meeting.

July 15th 1826   Rockingham City. VA
Dear Brother, I embrace the oppertunity to inform that the woll [whole] family is all well and hoping when these few lines come to hand they wil find you and yours quite the same. as for myself i am very pily [poorly] at this time we received the letter and with much sorrow we received it. brother Henry didint write anything to me or sister Nelly concerning sister Sally nor of her death i would be glad if you write to me concerning of her sickness and death whether she made her calling and election sure or not before she departed this life. i also desire to know where is her children and what you intend doing with them the 2 younges[t] especially because I can get good homes over here for them all. the woman that lived with me has departed and i have her baby also Nancey is with me but i will do the best i can for them. James and his family is all well except the baby. remember my love to misses clark and to sister betty and all the rest of my sisters and tell them to do the best they can for them poor little children. write to me immediately and let me know when the funeral [is] to be preacht. the 17th of agust camp meeting commences and i would be very glad if you and your wife could come and see me. no more at present but remain your affectionate sister untill death.

Frances Hackley

Besides her sisters Betty, Nelly, and Nancy, Fanny mentioned a number of other family members. "Brother Henry" may have been a relative or possibly the father of young Sarah's children. "James," also mentioned in John William Hackley's letter in 1819, was apparently the brother of Fanny's husband. "Misses Clark" was Hannah Clark, the mother of Willis's wife, Kitty.

Kitty's father, old William Clark, died in 1827, and his widow, Hannah, moved in with the Maddens, adding another member to the household. There were other additions: Willis and Kitty's children ––children to whom Willis taught the same lessons of growth, pride, and self-respect that his mother had taught him.

Willis and Kitty had two children by the time that Hannah Clark came to live with them. French was the older, born in 1825, and the new baby, Coleman, was born in 1827. (Seven more children were yet to be born: Samuel, born in 1829, Margretta, born around 1830, Sarah, in 1832; Mary, 1834; Maria, 1838; Jack, 1840; and Nathaniel, 1842.)

In the late 1820s Willis still did laborer's work when he had to, but he was also continuing with his blacksmithing, nail making, distilling business, and teamster work. The Maddens lived in rented dwellings during this time, mostly in a tenement—a rental house owned by William Lovell, a local merchant—somewhere around Stevensburg.

Know all men by these presents that we Willis Madden and John Bailey are held and firmly bound unto Uriel Terrill, committee of the estate of William Lovell in the just and full sum of forty dollars good and lawful money of Virginia to which payment well and truly to be made we bind ourselves our heirs executors and administrators jointly and severally firmly by these presents. Witness our hands and seals this third day of October one thousand eight hundred and twenty five.

The condition of this obligation is such that whereas Willis Madden and John Bailey have this day rented the tenement now in the possession of Mr. Madison Coleman, now if the above bound shall will and truly pay the just and full sum of Twenty dollars on the fifteenth day of November one thousand Eight Hundred and twenty six and deliver up the tenement at that time then the above obligation to be void otherwise to remain in full force and virtue

<pre>
                              his
Teste   Willis X
Jnº Ba [rest torn off]   [rest torn off]
                      John
</pre>

But no matter where their place of residence, they were always accompanied by the hidebound chest that held the family papers. Willis and Kitty were adding papers of their own to the family documents: business receipts, account papers, and notes for payment. Willis carefully tore his signature mark off each note as it was paid. The family papers trace the growth of Willis's business ventures during this time. A receipt from 1828–1829 shows that he bred a mare to a good stallion, Leopard. By 1833 he was paying taxes—six cents a head—on three horses, one of them probably the foal from his mare and Leopard. The tax list from the same year records the payment of his "levy"—the tax that like any free man, Negro or white, he owed on himself—in the amount of $1.05. And payments to local coach maker William Paul in 1833–1834, for repairs on Willis's two-horse wagon, tell of the success of his teamster business; Willis was getting so much work that he was actually wearing out his wagon.

> 1829 May 19th Received of Willis Madden by the hand of Wm G. Allen fifteen Shillings for the season of his mare to Leopard 1828
>
> Humphrey Hume

> Willis Maddins tax 1833
> To 1 levy 1.05   3 horses .18 $1.23

> 1833
> August 24th Recvd of Willis Madden twenty Seven Dollars in full for wood Work 2 horse Wagon
>
> Wm Paul

> Dec 14th 1834
> Recd of Willis Madden payment in full for wood work of two horse wagon
>
> Wm Paul

Other receipts speak of Willis's success in his distilling business. Among others, Albert G. Berry of Peola Mills, who had vouched for Willis's character in 1823, bought Willis's whiskey—in quantity:

> Willis Madden—please to send to me by Mr Byram 1 gallon and three quarts of your whiskey and oblige your friend
> Albert G. Berry

The most important papers Willis and Kitty Madden had, their registrations or "free papers," were not kept in the trunk. These they kept with them; they had to by law. These documents, complete with descriptions of the bearers, marking them as free and not slaves, had to be carried at all times by free Negroes. They might be required to produce these documents at any time, possibly by the county "patrols" that roamed the area to apprehend escaped slaves, slaves out without property passes, or free Negroes who were thought to be acting in a suspicious manner. Willis carried a duplicate set of free papers, issued to him after the loss or damage of his first papers. Kitty still had her original set, issued to her before she married, when she registered at the county courthouse upon reaching age twenty-one, as all free Negroes were required to do. The papers, including physical descriptions of their owners, are the only surviving images of the young couple:

State of Virginia

Persuant to an act of Assembly passed the 2nd day of March one thousand eight hundred and nineteen entitled "An act for reducing not one but several acts concerning slaves, free negroes and mulattoes" I Thomas Walker Lightfoot clerk of the County court of Culpeper in the state aforesaid do hereby certify that Willis Madden a dark mulatto man about twenty six years of age five foot six and a half inches high and born free is registered in my office agreeably to the directions of the above recited act

In Testimony whereof I have hereunto set my hand and seal this 19th day of September, one thousand

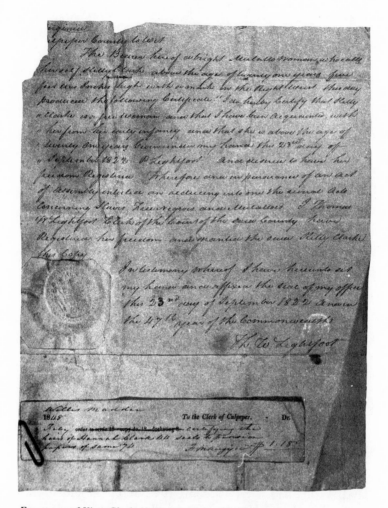

Free papers of Kitty Clark, Willis Madden's wife. This document was written on September 23, 1822.

eight hundred and twenty six in the 51st year of
the Commonwealth

T. W. Lightfoot

Virginia
Culpeper County to Wit

The Bearer hereof a bright Mulatto Woman who calls
herself Kitty Clark above the age of twenty one years five
feet two inches high with a mark on the Right Wrist this day
produced the following Certificate "I do hereby certify that
Kitty Clarke is a free Woman and that I have been Acquanted
with her from early infancy that that she is above the age of
twenty one years Given under my hand the 23rd day of
September 1822 P. Lightfoot" And desires to have her
freedom Registered. Wherefore and in persuance of an act
of Assembly entitled and reducing into one the several Acts
concerning Slaves Free Negroes and Mulattoes I Thomas
Walker Lightfoot Clerk of the Court of the said County have
Registered her freedom and granted the said Kitty Clarke
this Copy.

In Testimony whereof I have hereunto set my hand
and affixed the seal of my office this 23rd day of
September 1822 And in the 47th year of the Commonwealth

T. W. Lightfoot

By the mid-1830s life was going well for Willis. He had
a growing family, and his various businesses were beginning to prosper. He was realizing many of his ambitions.

But Willis had still another ambition. It concerned some
land. Willis had been watching the fate of the old Barnes
farm where his mother had lived and where she was buried.
The Barnes estate had been involved in a long chancery
case. Finally, in 1830, the land had been sold to a local man
named Frederick Cline. A few weeks later, perhaps by prior
agreement, Cline sold the land back to Robert Slaughter,
who had been executor of the estate. The property was thus
added to the Slaughter estate, The Grange. After Robert
Slaughter's death a few years later the entire estate, all twelve

On October 19, 1835, Willis purchased from Martin Slaughter the eighty-seven-acre parcel of land that would eventually expand to an estate of more than one thousand acres. The transaction was recorded on a handwritten document of three pages.

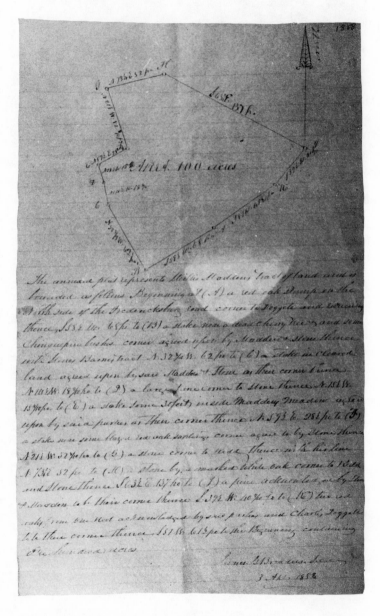

Plot of the Madden farm drawn up in 1858.

hundred acres of The Grange, was sold at auction to another member of the family, Martin Slaughter.

In late 1835 Madden approached Martin Slaughter with an offer for the old Barnes farm. Slaughter was interested. He had two large tracts besides the Barnes land, which, at eighty-seven acres, was by far the smallest parcel; moreover, the soil on the Barnes tract was poor. Martin Slaughter and Madden were discussing prices of less than $3 an acre when good farmland was selling for $15 to $30 an acre. Madden would end up raising rocks more than likely, and he was willing to pay for the privilege. When the bargaining was finished, Madden had bought the land for $2.50 an acre. His deed is dated the thirteenth day of October 1835, and before a week passed, he had carried the precious document to the courthouse and had it officially recorded. He was now the owner of a hardscrabble farm, a derelict house, and a lonely grave under the oak trees—his past and his future.

Chapter Five

MADDEN'S TAVERN

❦

1. *Any person who shall, for compensation, furnish lodging or diet to a person boarding in his house, or provender for a horse feeding in his stable or on his land, (except a drove of live stock, and persons attending it,) and sell by retail wine or ardent spirits, or a mixure thereof, to be drank in or at the place of sale, shall be deemed to keep an ordinary or house of public entertainment.*

2. *Any person who shall, for a time not exceeding one month, if within, or not exceeding one week, if without a city of town, furnish for compensation lodging or diet to one boarding in his house, or provender for a horse feeding in his stable or on his land, except as aforesaid, shall, if he be not the keeper of an ordinary, according to the preceeding section, be deemed to keep a house of private entertainment, unless the place of furnishing the same, when without a city or town, be more than eight hundred yards from a public road or highway.*

Code of Virginia, 1849

Willis Madden was now a landowner. The fact must have called for a celebration in the family. While there are no details about this event, there is no doubt that the purchase of the land was accompanied by pride and rejoicing. Perhaps Willis even acquired a small souvenir to commemorate the day. In the fall of 1982 I found near the house a penny dated 1835, the year that he bought the land. The initials *W* and *M* had been scratched into the coin. Was this a keepsake made for Willis Madden on the occasion of his becoming a landowner?

The family legends tell that Willis had made plans for the farm even before he actually owned it. Years before, he had watched the traffic passing on the roads that crossed near the old Barnes house. The roads—rutted ribbons of dirt and rocks winding through the countryside, rivers of mud in winter and spring, filled with choking clouds of dust in summer and autum—weren't easy to travel, but they were the lifelines of travel and trade for the region. The major routes from north to south and east to west came together right there in a series of great crossroads.

There was the old Fredericksburg Road, or Kirtley Road (from Culpeper to Fredericksburg), the Peola Mills–Kellysville Road (from Sperryville in Rappahannock County, through Madison County to Culpeper County), and the Stony Ford Road (to Brandy Station and then north into Fauquier County), with many smaller roads feeding into these highways. These roads and their extensions connected all the main routes in that section of the country. East of the crossroads, the Richardsville and Eley's Ford roads continued on toward Fredericksburg, still the center of trade for the region. On foot, by horseback, and in wagons they came, travelers and teamsters passing by. They came from the whole western Piedmont, funneling down to the crossroads—from western Culpeper, Madison, Rappahannock, Fauquier counties, even the Shenandoah Valley, from the whole upcountry, or "uppercutter" as people called it.

The land where Sarah Madden had lived, the land that Willis Madden had now purchased, stood just at these crossroads. It was one day's travel outside Fredericksburg

Tax receipts for Willis Madden's farm for the years 1850, 1855, 1862, and for the postwar years 1866 and 1867.

and, for many of the travelers, just one day's journey from their homes farther up the country.

Willis Madden's farm was right at the beginning of the Great Fork or Chinquapin Neck, a narrow neck of land in the fork of the Rappahannock and the Rapidan rivers, which made up the eastern portion of Culpeper County. The Neck, as it was called locally, was all the land east of a line from Fox's Neck on the Rapidan northward through Lignum to Kellysville at Kelly's Ford on the Rappahannock. It was a region of notoriously poor land, yielding a poor living. Its best crops were timber and products gathered from wild plants: chinquapins—the chestnutlike nuts of the chinquapin bush—and peth—the root bark from sassafras, which was processed for seasoning and oil. "Chinquapin Neck," ran the old rhyme, "land of peth—one half lived and the other half starved to death!"

The farm wasn't the best land, and Willis knew this from the beginning, but then he hadn't planned on just farming. At first he worked at improving the land and raising food for his family, while he continued his teamster business and his other work. But he had other plans. Willis Madden knew that this land, *his land*, at the crossroads—at the halfway point between Fredericksburg and the areas that were dependent on Fredericksburg for trade and the selling of their produce—was a natural place for a tavern.

It is never an easy thing to set up a business, and for Willis Madden it was harder than for most. In addition to the work that was required, there were other considerations for Willis Madden. He was, after all, a free Negro.

In the first years of the new American Republic, Virginia had codified its laws concerning slaves and free Negroes. The statutes became law in 1792, a few years before Willis was born. The old restrictions on free Negroes were repeated and strengthened. Some threatened slave rebellions around this time, such as the unsuccessful Gabriel's Insurrection in 1800, occasioned fears among Virginia's whites concerning both slaves and free Negroes. But these worries had calmed during the next thirty years, when virtually no slave uprisings occurred. Willis Madden had grown up during an era of relaxing attitudes toward slaves and free Negroes in Virginia. Enforcement of laws restricting free Negroes was often lax, and some state legislators spoke of eliminating slavery entirely. But all this changed after the bloody Nat Turner Rebellion in Southampton County in 1831. There was no more talk in the state government of ending slavery.

Although few free Negroes took part in slave revolts and no free Negroes were ever among the ringleaders, the white population, terrified by the prospects of slave revolts, considered free Negroes potential leaders and rallying points for rebellions. Increasingly restrictive laws against Negroes, both slave and free, were passed, and earlier laws, already in effect but often not enforced, began to be strictly applied.

The new Code of Virginia, enacted after the Nat Turner Rebellion, contained the largest and most detailed collection of "Black Laws" yet assembled in Virginia; the list went on for pages. Besides the expended slave codes, there were new and more severe restrictions on free Negroes: Free Negroes could no longer be legally educated in Virginia; they were often forbidden to move to another location within the state; they could no longer own any sort of gun or "military weapon," even for hunting. One of the Madden family stories recounts that Willis Madden once had to use a wooden pole to kill a rabid dog that threatened to attack his children, since the law did not allow him to have a weapon.

Under the new laws Negroes, whether free or enslaved, could no longer legally hold meetings, religious or otherwise, without whites being present, and no Negroes could conduct such a meeting. This had the effect of outlawing Negro preachers, slave or free. Negroes were no longer allowed trial by jury except in the case of capital crimes, and the punishments that the law prescribed for Negroes convicted of certain crimes were more severe than those given to whites.

The laws reflected fears of Negro revolts and crimes, but there was also another fear: that of Negro success. By the 1830s many trades were being carried on mainly by Negroes. An 1831 petition to the Virginia legislature, signed by more than one hundred Culpeper citizens, cited Negro-dominated trades such as blacksmithing, shoemaking, masonry, plastering, milling, and carpentry and demanded that Negroes, both slave and free, be prohibited from serving as apprentices or learning trades, to prevent competition with white tradesmen.

But while this and other petitions were circulating in Virginia, complaining of the industriousness of these Negro tradesmen and seeking to bar them from many trades, still other petitions took a different direction: to drive free Negroes from the state. Complaints stated that Negroes were the most shiftless and degraded members of society—unwilling to work, burdens on the counties where they lived, petty criminals. An 1846 petition from Culpeper County, signed by over eighty county citizens, requested the state legislature to remove all free Negroes from Culpeper County—not because of their industry but because of their laziness and tendency to crime. A similar petition in 1852 demanded the removal of all free Negroes from Virginia. Although none of these petitions became law, the fears and attitudes that produced them were widespread. One writer of the time spoke for many whites when he declared that "Taken as a whole class . . . they [free Negroes] must be considered the most worthless and indolent of the citizens of the United States. It is well known that throughout the whole extent of our union they are looked upon as the very drones and pests of society."

Willis Madden was walking a tightrope. Ambitious by nature, he was intent on setting up his own business and determined to succeed in life. Yet he was restricted by law and cut off from the company of most other Negroes. But Willis also had his pride, his native intelligence, and his belief in himself. Where another man might never have tried at all, Willis Madden not only tried but went ahead and succeeded.

During the first years that he owned the farm, Willis spent most of his time renewing the neglected fields and repairing and constructing buildings. He cleared off a wagonyard several acres in size and dug a deep well in the middle of it. He built a general store and a blacksmith and wheelwright shop on the premises. Anything that the travelers or teamsters who stayed on his land might need could be found right there.

Although his property had quickly become known as Madden's tavern, Willis was basically running a camping ground for the teamsters and drovers who passed by his house. Laws against Negroes selling liquor and running taverns (or ordinaries, as they were sometimes called) were becoming increasingly restrictive. By the time Willis set up his business he was already limited in what he could legally do. The 1830 Code of Virginia forbade any Negro from selling liquor within one mile of any sort of "public assembly"; by 1853 the keeping of any sort of tavern was, by law, a business closed to Negroes. But it was also a commonplace occurrence in those days for farmers to give food and shelter to travelers, who then paid their hosts. If one did this on a steady basis, a license to provide "private entertainment"—as opposed to the "public entertainment" of a tavern—might be required. In fact, few licenses for taverns or places of "private entertainment" were actually issued in Culpeper County; there was a heavy tax on these licenses, and a bond was also required. Most people preferred to point out that they only took in an occasional traveler or were just allowing teamsters and drovers to camp on their property

*In the woods near Germanna, Virginia, can be found stretches of the old road
from Fredericksburg, first cut in 1714 during Governor Alexander Spotswood's
term of office. Weary travelers on this highway found a haven of comfort at
Madden's tavern. Courtesy Moss Publications.*

(which the law permitted without a license) and thus were
not really running a tavern or similar operation. Willis
Madden belonged to this group; only a few travelers, all
described as his "friends," actually stayed in his house,
according to the "official" story. The campground was the
main part of his business, and of course, the teamsters usually supplied their own food and drink. Willis Madden merely
rented them a campground and supplied some provisions
and services when necessary.

In truth, the campground *was* the mainstay of Willis's
business, but far more business was going on in the house
than he would or could admit. Many of his customers visited Madden's tavern repeatedly, men like John P. Kelly,
who owned the mill at Kelly's Ford on the Rappahannock
River, several miles northeast of Willis's farm. Traveling on
business, Kelly stayed at Madden's tavern once a week dur-

ing the two months between late April and late June 1844. His accounts, listing him as "Detter [debtor] to Willis Madden," record that his horses were fed several gallons of grain at each stay, while Kelly himself always received "3 meals of victuals."

Willis Madden's house served as both a tavern and a gathering place for the neighborhood, and Willis also supplied a variety of liquors, something he was not (and, as a Negro, later *could* not be) licensed to do. According to Madden family legend, Willis Madden didn't sell his liquor since he had no license to retail spirits. His liquor was "free," costs being added to the price of meals served with the drinks. Only a very few receipts from the family records show Willis charging for liquor, although there are numerous bills showing that he bought large quantities of several varieties of whiskey. William Warren's company in Fredericksburg, which specialized in liquors, was Willis's main supplier. Willis bought it by the barrel (each barrel contained thirty-six to forty gallons), his bills listing "Family Rye Whiskey," "Old Rye Whiskey," "Rectified Whiskey," "Common Whiskey."

This typical business account, showing purchases for Willis Madden's tavern and store from William Warren, Jr.'s company in Fredericksburg, dates from the early 1850s:

Mr. Willis Madden
Bot of Wm. Warren, Jr.
1853

Jany	29	1	Barrel Family Rye Whiskey 36 gals @ 50			18.00
		1	Loaf Sugar	12 lb	10	1.20
	30		lb Brown Sugar @ 60			2.50
	30		lb Coffee @ 11			3.33
	1		Box Cigars			1.00
Feby	19	1	Bundle Hoop Iron 5 lbs @ 6 1/4			.31
Apl	25	1	Barrel Old Rye Whiskey 36 gals @ 50			18.00

10		lb Sugar @ 6d 83 10 lb Coffee @ 11c 1.10		1.93
28	1	Tierce Washington Lime		1.25
Aug 17	1	Barrel Herrings		5.75
Sept 24	1	Barrel Common Whiskey 36 gals @ 33c		11.88
	2	Gals Molasses @ 2/3		.75
Octo 3	10	lb Coffee 14c 1.40 1 Barrel Herrings 5.75		7.15
8	56	lb Bacon @ 12		6.72
Nov 30	1	barrel Rectified Whiskey 39 1/2 gals @ 35c		13.82
1854				
Febry 15	1	Sack Salt		2.25
Mar 20	1	Barrel Common Whiskey 36 gals @ 36c		12.96
Mar 20	1	Barrel Common Whiskey 36 gals @ 34c		13.09
				121.89

Credits

1853

Febry 19	By 1 Dry Hide 22 lb @ 10c	2.20	
Sept 20	" Cash at Culpeper Court House	25.00	
1854			
Augt 10	" Cash in Fredericksburg	50.00	77.20
	Balance	44.69	

1854

Aug 10	To 1 Barrel Herrings	6.25
	" 49 lb Bacon @ 12 1/2	6.12
	" 1 Barrel Common Whiskey 40 gals @ 36c	14.40
		71.46

Legend has it that Madden's tavern was once visited by a group of men who were jealous of Willis's success. According to one version, they were disgruntled tavern owners who were losing too much business to him. The visitors were intent on trapping Willis into selling liquor, which would mean he was running an unlicensed tavern. Ushered into the house, they were given glass after glass of whiskey. At the end of the evening they demanded their bill. Willis, looking suitably puzzled for the occasion, declared that he was just hosting his "friends," as all his other customers were also described, and of course, he would never charge his friends for his hospitality. As the men were leaving, the ringleader half-jokingly told Willis that they had been out to "catch" him. Willis, who had been on to the plan all the time, replied, with a set smile, that "catchin's just before hangin'!"

By law Willis Madden was indeed committing a crime by running his tavern, yet his was among the most respectable and well-run establishments in the county and was patronized by county officials and other important men in the area. They could have prosecuted Willis Madden; instead, faced with the loss of a popular and convenient stopping place, they looked the other way. If Willis Madden chose to extend his hospitality to "friends" who happened by, and if those same friends, in an equally neighborly fashion, chose to reimburse him, although never, of course, for his free whiskey, then what of it?

As his reputation and business increased, Willis turned his attention to the house. The Barnes house, nearly seventy years old and deteriorating, was completely unsuited for Willis's family and business needs. Repairs, even additions, Willis realized, were only stopgap measures. He set about planning and building a new house, the one he wanted.

A site was cleared, facing the road yet well back from it. Stakes were driven to mark the corners of the house, aligned to the four points of the compass.

Willis and his sons hauled rocks for the chimneys and foundation, stone that they had probably already stockpiled when they were clearing the neglected fields. There would be no cellar; storage and cooking would be done in the outbuildings and in the separate outside kitchen building that they had already constructed. After the stone foundation of the house was laid, the walls were raised. They were not of frame but of logs, hewn flat on each wall surface and notched at the corners to be held in place. Stronger than frame, the log walls also provided more of the natural insulation of the wood. The spaces between the logs were chinked, or filled with a mixture of stones and slats of wood. The chinking was then daubed, or sealed with clay intermixed with animal hair or chopped straw as a binder—a chore that even the youngest children could help with. The roof was supported by a framework of rafters made from the trunks of small pines or cedars, over which were nailed rough, wide boards. Finally the roof was covered with shingles that Willis and his sons had split by hand, fitting them snugly against the large stone chimneys that were rising, one from each end of the house.

It was a medium-size, rather than large, house. A plain house, but solid and comfortable: two rooms on the ground floor, two rooms in the loft above. The wide floorboards were cut at one of the nearby sawmills, along with the weatherboards that were to cover the outside walls, both to imitate the more finished look of a frame house and to make the building more weathertight. The inside walls were whitewashed to keep the rooms clean and brighter than they would have been with just the dark log walls. Each room had its own fireplace—the only heat available—and for several of the rooms Willis made simple mantels, modeled on the classical pieces in the larger houses in the area.

The building was divided into two sections. The family lived in half of the house and kept the other half for the public. The upstairs of the public section was usually occupied by travelers as a sleeping room. Downstairs was the tavern room, the gathering place where both travelers and local people could visit, have food and drink, and talk—about business, politics, and anything else.

Of course, most of the people who stopped at Madden's tavern never stayed *in* the house. These were the teamsters and drovers. The wagonyard, which stood in front of the house, covered three acres. The people who drove stock—cattle, hogs, and even turkeys were driven to market on foot in those days—or who brought wagonloads of goods back and forth to Fredericksburg slept in the open around their campfires or under their wagons, their stock grazing nearby.

Willis was already prospering in the first years after he bought his land. He was able to build his new house in 1840, and by early 1841 he had paid off the purchase money on his land as well. As he had done with his original deed, Willis carried the release of his mortgage to the courthouse to be properly recorded. But if there had been good times before, the years that followed—the rest of the 1840s and the early 1850s—were the boom times for Madden's tavern. Trade was heavy, teamsters and travelers being plentiful. Willis was managing a large, busy operation, combining several different trades and businesses. Several of his sons, as well as nephews and other relatives, were working for him. There was never any shortage of things for them to do.

A receipt from 1842 shows that business was already so good that Willis was buying forage from surrounding farmers to feed the teamsters' and drovers' stock:

> 22nd of November, 1842. Received of Willis Madden, a free man, the sum of five dollars, being payment for a thousand weight of hay gotten by his nephews Burgess and Willis, last spring.
>
> George Hamilton, jr.

The thousand pounds of hay was bought from George Hamilton, who owned a plantation nearby. Today moving hay in bales with a truck or tractor is a simple job. But back then, when hay was stored in stacks and moved with hay knives and pitchforks, it was a tremendous undertaking to get a half ton of hay into wagons, drive it miles down a rutted country road, and then restack it. The short note probably reflected several days' work for Willis's nephews to get the hay and for Willis and the other workers to help them unload and stack it at the tavern.

Besides running the tavern and campground, Willis farmed and continued his teamster business. On his frequent trips to Fredericksburg to pick up or sell his own supplies and produce, he often carried items for other people in the area as well. Hauling wagonloads of produce or building materials and doing contracting jobs wherever needed were also lucrative parts of his business. Some clients, such as the local doctor Robert Wellford, hired Willis for teamster work and also stayed in the tavern. William B. Ross, who sent several loads of shingles to the county seat on Willis's wagons, also sold him guano (fertilizer).

1852	Mr Robert Wellford	
	To Willis Madden	Dr [debit]
April 27th for hawling goods up		$2 00
May 27 hawling 1 load of plank [to] steam mill		2 50
August 5th hawling 1 load of plank		2 00
1853 Feb 2nd to servant & 2 horses all night		0 0
supper & breakfast for servant		
& feed for the horses		1 50
1856 Feb 5th to servant and two horses all night		0 0
supper and breakfast for servant		
& feed for the horses		1 50
		$9.50

Mr Wm. B. Ross	Dr [debit]
to Willis Madden	
To hawling 1 load of Shingle to the Court House	4 00
To hawling 13 thousand 113 at 50 cts a thousand	6 55
	10 55

> received of Mr Ross in cash $5   <u>5</u>
> November 4th 1854 paid French Madden   5 55
> Twenty Dollars for guano received of Mr Ross
> Willis Madden

Willis also acted somewhat as an employment agency for the free Negroes of the neighborhood, providing skilled, reliable workers to a number of employers throughout the region. Among other businesses, Willis supplied men to work in the local gold mines (before the California gold strike of 1849 central Virginia was the largest gold-producing region in the United States). When James Richards made one such request in 1843, he addressed it to "Mr. Willis Madden" and directed his messenger, a Mr. Wentz, to read the letter to Willis, who was unable to read for himself.

Mr. Willis Madden
    If Mr. Willis Madden can send down two hands to work on a surface mine he will greatly
> Oblige
> James Richards
> 19th May 1843
    Mr. Wentz will oblige J. Richards by reading the above to W. Madden

The scope of Willis's business did not reduce the amount of work at the tavern and his farm. At home, fields had to be worked and kept up, and harvests gathered in. Willis grew corn and hay—fodder for his animals and for the livestock of his travelers. His orchards produced fruit that was eaten fresh in the spring and summer, dried for the winter, or made into brandy. More corn was grown, destined for the family's and tavern's tables as corn pones, hominy, and corn bread. And there were fields of wheat waving around the tavern, the ripe grains were sold or traded to the merchants whom Willis dealt with. Besides the crops, there was the tavern and the yard and shops to be taken care of.

The Madden family stories still speak of the workday that started before dawn. Long before the sun began to peep over the horizon, the family was already awake. The women had started to prepare breakfast in the kitchen building behind the tavern, cooking in the open fireplace. Willis, his sons, and the other workers were already on their way to the shops near the wagonyard. The drovers and teamsters were awake, too, cooking their breakfasts over campfires, gathering their stock, hitching up their teams. The air was alive with the sounds of men and animals; curses, shouts, jokes, and conversation blended with the noises of the livestock. The store was open for business, and supplies were sold. The forge was fired up to make any needed repairs. Horseshoes, wheel rims, wagon hardware, harness—Willis could mend them all. Soon the wagons were packed and turning out onto the dusty road, heading to their destinations. It was still barely daybreak.

Travelers who were staying in the tavern could rise a little later and eat a big country breakfast served by Kitty Madden before they headed on. The smells from the kitchen were tantalizing—and the eating even better. From the pots, Dutch ovens, and grills over the fire came sausage and ham from the Madden hogs, fresh eggs from Kitty's chickens, coffee, and hominy. And there was crackling bread or corn pones, wrapped in cabbage leaves and baked in the ashes until they were golden brown. Any traveler who left Madden's tavern hungry had only himself to blame.

After the drovers and other travelers were on the road, the wagonyards and shops had to be cleaned. Taverns often had a reputation for being dirty places, and Willis Madden would tolerate no untidiness in his. After the farm chores were finished, the work crews then scattered—to the fields, to do other work on the place, to haul goods or get supplies. The general store was kept open most of the day, since it was also a supply center for the neighborhood. His business receipts show the range and completeness of his store. Willis Madden didn't stock just a few bolts of cloth; his store displayed or was able to get within a few days silk, calico, ribbons, "green gingham," "summer muslin" and "check[ed] muslin," linen, "white lawn," cotton, and the coarser kersey. There were staples: coffee, sugar, salt, shoes, molasses, knives and forks, needles, pins, and thread. Fancier things also appear on Willis's orders: "a gold ring," china cups and saucers, a set of teaspoons. And there was no shortage of hats in Willis Madden's store: wool hats, straw hats, "a sealskin Cap," "Panama hats."

By evening other travelers were coming in, or perhaps one or two had stayed over, doing business in the neighborhood. They met in the downstairs tavern room. For dinner Kitty would make ham and fried chicken, corn bread, boiled greens, and sweet potatoes from the garden. Sometimes she served imported herrings that Willis brought up from Fredericksburg and maybe little "Irish" (white) potatoes. Since Madden's tavern was a gathering place for local people as well, the travelers often were joined by men from the neighborhood. Willis's fine "free" whiskey, some of it made on the premises, still more brought from Fredericksburg, was always on hand, and the men ate, drank, and talked far into the evening.

The Fredericksburg whiskey was a drawing card for Madden's tavern. In fact, Willis brought most of his supplies from Fredericksburg. It was still the major trading center for the region, with better selections and prices than Willis could find farther "up the country." He had credit with several of the merchants there, such as William Warren, "Wholesale and Retail Dealer in Teas, Wines, Cigars and Choice Liquors," and Scott, French & Co., "Produce and Comission Merchants and dealers in Groceries, Guano, Agricultural Implements &c."

Among the papers in Willis's trunk was a short letter written by William G. Allen, one of the local farmers who

Receipt from the William Warren, Jr., Company of Fredericksburg, Virginia, dated February 26, 1855, attests to the character of Willis Madden. Willis's credit was obviously excellent in the business community. The receipt closes with "Anything you want let me know" and is signed "Your friend Wm. Warren Jr." Scores of such papers were found in the family trunk.

had vouched for Willis's character and helped prevent the breakup of Sarah's family. The note, addressed to Mrs. Mary Stevens (a major landowner in eastern Culpeper County and daughter-in-law of General Edward Stevens, for whom Stevensburg was named), recommended Willis's work as an honest "Black Boy":

> The bearer Willis Madden is a free Boy under [humble] as a Caracter as any Black Boy in Virginia. I have nown him for twenty years and he has been helping me of[f] and On for ten or twelve years. He can give satisfaction as Relates

to his Honesty by a numerous persons he is very Industrus and well behav. ^d to all persons.

> Wm. G. Allen
> 7th Sept. 1827

Willis Madden was twenty-eight years old at the time, and it was the white custom to address Negroes as "boys" until old age, when they then became "uncles." Willis Madden was not old enough to be an "uncle," but he was a "boy" no longer. He now received letters and business correspondence addressed "Sir," "Willis Madden, Esquire," "Mister Willis Madden"—courtesies rarely extended to a Negro. In a time when most Negroes were treated as inferiors, Willis's correspondence was in the form of polite exchanges and discussion of business services, worded to make it clear that he was an equal in the business world.

Feby 26th 1855
Mr. Willis Madden
1 Barrel Whiskey 34 ½ gals. 42 [cents]   14.49
Credit
By Cash on account through Billy   10.00
Dear Willis:
I send you a Barrel of good whiskey at 42 cts. This Whiskey cost me 41 cts., so I make only one cent on the gallon. I will send you your Account by mail to Stevensburg to shew you how we stand. I would have sent it to you before, but I thought you might think I was dunning you. You know I told you I was not going to ask you for any money. But you know whenever you send any, it is very acceptable. Anything you want let me know.

> Your friend
> Wm. Warren Jr.

To Willis Madden
     Sir
          Mrs Barnes wagoner Abram will leave with you 10 bags of Clover Seed and Timothy Seeds, also a letter for my overseer Mr Yancey. You must send the letter up to my

house immediately by one of your boys and Mr Yancey will send my wagon down for it. Keep the 10 Bags carefully in your house till Mr Yancey sends for them. Send your boy up immediately on the arrival of the wagon to my house with the letter for Mr Yancey. I will pay you when I come up.

> Yours,
> Wm H. Wellford
> Saturday March 6, 1847

[To] Willis Madden Esq.
Culpeper City   Virginia
Stevensburg April 30th 1852
Willis Madden
        Bought of Thos Rees Jr.
To ½ barrel corn meal @ 60c $1.50
I will take it as a great favour if you would take your waggon and go to Fredericksburg and get me a load of goods at William Warrens   I will pay you 35 cents per hundred

> Thos Rees Jr.
> By J. D. Rees

Willis Madden's honesty and integrity were unquestioned. As a tavern keeper Willis had access to his guests' money and weapons, indication of the high esteem and trust accorded him by the white community. He was frequently asked to deliver messages, even money, to various people, and he often acted as a go-between in business or disputes between Negroes and whites. His ambitions had become reality. He had come up from a laborer to a man of property and substance, one who was respected by both the Negro and white communities. Willis continued to be regarded as the head of the Madden clans in Culpeper: his own family, the families of his sisters, and others to which the Maddens were related. He was now well known throughout that end of Culpeper, and his reputation extended into the neighboring counties. This unquestioned integrity was a far cry from the days when he needed references to prove his honesty. Willis Madden now appeared in court himself, to be the reference or security for his friends and relatives. He had appeared as the sole reference—"a man of credit and honesty and his word to be depended upon," the official record said—for old Hannah Clark, Kitty's mother, when she claimed the revolutionary pension due her late husband. Willis had even appeared in court to petition the county to reroute old roads or open new roads which would be more convenient to his business, and his requests had been granted.

[Culpeper County Minute Book 21]
p. 234 [October 21, 1845] On the motion of Willis Madden for leave to change the road from the Paoli Mills to the Richmond Road where the same runs through the land of the said Madden, ordered that one or more of the comrs [commissioners] of roads of this county view and report
p. 264 [March 16, 1846] On the petition of Willis Madden for a road. The report of Chas. Jones one of the road comrs was returned and ordered to be filed
p. 274 [April 30, 1846] On the petition of Willis Madden for a road . . . ordered that the road be changed according to the report of Charles Jones, one of the road comrs.

By the early 1850s Madden's tavern was one of the leading establishments operating between Fredericksburg and Culpeper. The food and drink that Willis served were top-notch; the quality had not suffered with his success. And besides providing for overnight guests, the tavern was a landmark and more than ever a gathering place for the men of the neighborhood.

Chapter Six

DECLINE AND WAR

To the Legislature of Virginia the undersigned beg leave respectfully to represent—That the large increase of that portion of the population of the County of Culpeper, known as "free persons of Colour," of late, has created a grievance which they think ought to be removed—indeed unless it can to some extent be relieved, it is difficult to tell what will be the condition of the white people. Free negroes congregate in and about our little Towns and by idleing their time indeed entirely neglecting to work they show no visible means of support, and must steal or perish. The great number of slaves in Culpeper (more numerous at the last Census than the whites) furnish them very readily with the means of obtaining supplies at the expense of the industruous farmers and mechanics. Your laws to restrain free negroes though kindly intended to prevent their robbing the whites through their slaves, fails entirely to effect that object, and we are satisfied that no legislation will relieve us of the evil of which we complain, that falls short of giving us the power to send them from our County at our own expense. We your petitioners therefore ask your honorable body to pass a law authorizing the county court of Culpeper to lay a county levy for the purpose of defraying the expense of sending the free Negroes of Culpeper without the bounds of the state. Your petitioners have stated the grievance under which in common with their countrymen in general they labour and their full conviction that it cannot be relieved but by sending free negroes away, *and propose to do that at their own expense. As to the details of a bill to effect that object, they willingly and cheerfully leave that to the wisdom and justice of your honr. body and in duty they will ever &c.*

Legislative Petition, January 10, 1846 (signed by seventy-seven Culpeper citizens)

To the Honerable the Senate & House of Representatives of the Commonwealth of Va. in general Assembly met—The petition of the subscribers citizens of Culpeper state of Va. Prayeth—that a law be passed at this session for the removal of Free blacks from the commonwealth of Va.—and as one mode of getting shut of them at as little expense as possible we humbly pray that as many of them as wish to remain in the state be suffered to sell themselves to masters of their choice, and your petitioners further pray that a law be passed making any contract with them before some officer of the law obligatory on them—and your petitioners as in duty bound will ever pray &c.

Legislative Petition, February 21, 1852 (signed by thirty-one Culpeper citizens)

The 1850 Census shows Willis Madden as the head of a large family. Besides Willis and Kitty, six children were still at home: Coleman, aged twenty-three; Sarah Ann, eighteen; Mary, sixteen; Maria, twelve; Jack, ten; and Nathaniel (always called Nat), eight. Also living with the family, working on the farm, and involved with Willis's other business ventures were William Clark, Kitty's brother, and Samuel and William Hackley, apparently Willis's nephews. French Madden, aged twenty-five, still lived in Culpeper County but at some distance from his parents. Samuel and Margretta had left the area.

1850 Census, Culpeper County
[p. 249]

Willis Madden, 51, black male, farmer (Head of Household)
Kitty Madden, 50, mulatto female
Coleman Madden, 23, mulatto male
Sarah A. Madden, 18, mulatto female
Mary F. Madden, 16, mulatto female
Maria Madden, 12, mulatto female
Jack Madden, 10, mulatto male
Nathaniel Madden, 8, mulatto male
William Clark, 60, mulatto male, laborer
Samuel Hackley, 40, black male, laborer
William Hackley, 30, mulatto male, laborer

Samuel had moved north, away from the restrictions of
Virginia law, and was a minister in Baltimore. An early
letter to his parents, preserved among the family papers,
shows that soon after he left home and arrived in the city,
he was fighting an illness—or was it homesickness?

Baltimore June 5th 1850
Dear Father & Mother   I take my pen in hand to inform
you that I am not very Well at present   I have Been unwell
for the Last 2 or 3 Weeks and for about 9 days I have Been
quite sick in fact for 2 or 3 days was not able to do any thing
But am Better now I hope these few Lines May find you
enjoying good health and happiness Love to sisters & Brothers friends relations & acquaintances Mr. Ball & family Will
Come home next week & I want to Come home in a Bout 2
weeks if I Can get off and go to the springs to spend the
summer   But it will [be] verry hard for Mee to get off I
know But if I get no Better nor no worse I Must get off if
nothing happens dont Bee uneasy I am not verry sick I shall
write again soon if nothing happens I have given you all the
news I have that is worth sending I must now Close good
night
I remain your affectionate son untill death
Write soon

                                        S W Madden

Willis Madden's business was now at its height. Culpeper County tax records for the 1840s and early 1850s show

Elegant mantel clock with metal works, purchased by Willis Madden in Fredericksburg, Virginia, in the late 1840s. A symbol of affluence, the clock was one of Willis's prized possessions. Photo, Stephen W. Sylvia.

that he was the wealthiest free Negro in the area. He had expanded his farming and teamster operations; in most years he kept a stable of four or five horses and owned from twenty to fifty cows and hogs. His livestock and his household furniture were far more extensive—and worth far more—than those of many of the county's whites.

Among Willis's possessions was a "metallic" clock—a small clock with metal works, not the wooden works often seen at the time. Acquired in the late 1840s, the clock must have come up from Fredericksburg on one of Willis's wagons. From the county tax records we know that for many years Willis was the only Negro in the county with such a clock.

It remained a prized possession throughout his life and then a treasured heirloom in his family. I'm looking at it as I write these lines.

Willis was unique among Culpeper Negroes, and most whites as well, for yet another reason: He had had his photograph made—possibly at the county seat or on a trip to Fredericksburg. The photograph and the clock stood side by side on Willis's mantel, luxuries enough for most white families in Culpeper at the time but unheard of for free Negroes. Willis had everything: success, respect, and prosperity. And with each stroke of the clock, it came a little bit nearer to the end.

Photographic carte de visite *taken in the 1850s reveals a handsome and prosperous Willis Madden in the prime of life.*

After the mid-1850s things were never the same for Willis Madden or for his tavern. His life up to that point had been a success story, built of hard work and struggle. Now Willis Madden's fortune turned against him. Through no fault of his own, a number of events came together and began his decline.

The Orange and Alexandria Railroad had come through Culpeper County in 1852, connecting the area with northern Virginia. Willis's son French Madden, along with several of the Bannisters, had worked on the railroad crew. But ironically, the same railroad that provided French Madden with a temporary job forever changed travel and trade in the region and signaled the begining of the end of his father's business. Few people from the region were willing to haul their goods all the way to Fredericksburg when their shipping could be done by train, either from Brandy Station, only a few miles northwest of Madden's tavern, or right from the town of Culpeper. Some people from the area still traded in Fredericksburg, the tavern was still a gathering place for the neighborhood, and a few travelers still stopped there; but the old days of the drovers and the campground were dying.

Willis had to rely more on his store and shops, on farming, and on short hauling trips around the neighborhood for income. But there was less money coming in now to keep the store well stocked, and fewer people were coming in to buy. And Willis was getting too old for hard farm work; in 1859 he would be sixty years old. He was still "Mr. Willis Madden" in business correspondence, but with his whitening hair, he was now "Uncle Willis" to most of his customers.

Nor was there much help around home for Willis. Many of his relatives had died, and he had always encouraged his children to rise in the world, to think of horizons beyond the borders of the farm. Many of them had learned to read and write, an advantage that Willis never had. But there was danger in acquiring an education: It was illegal for any white to teach a Negro, slave or free, to read or write, so the young Maddens were taught secretly, probably by sympathetic neighbors. Opportunities for Willis's children in Culpeper County were limited. Some, such as Samuel and Margretta, had already gone away to seek their fortunes. Others had remained in Culpeper, trying to work around the system, as Willis had done. Willis's son French, a millwright, master of the massive framing and machinery then used to construct mills, was still living in Culpeper County, along with Nat, the youngest boy. Both of them, however, were engaged in their own work; neither lived at home.

By the end of the decade only Willis's son Jack was still with his parents. Help had gotten harder to find, and Willis had finally hired a slave from one of his neighbors to make sure that he got his crops planted and his harvest in. The lease was to run from early 1857 until Christmas 1858—a period of almost two years during which Willis apparently had no other sure prospects for an extra farmhand. As was usual for anyone who hired a slave, Willis had to give bond for the conditions of the lease and the proper treatment of the slave.

Bond   Willis Madden
I have hired from William Redd for the present year a slave named Jeff to be employed on my farm in this county [Culpeper] for the present year for farming purposes. In consideration whereof I bind myself my heirs etc. to pay sd. Redd his heirs etc. the sum of Sixty dollars for his hire on the 1st day of January next ensuing and permit him to return to the said Redd on the 25th day of December next well clothed & shod and in the mean time to furnish him with the usual summer clothing. Given under my hand & seal this 1st March 1857.

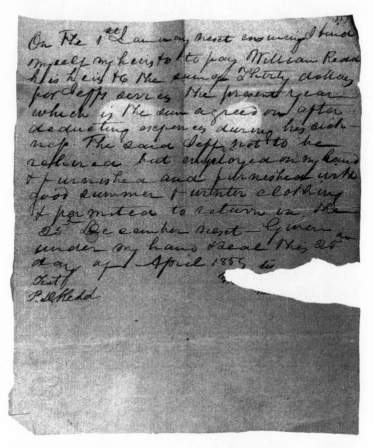

This rare document written in 1859 is Willis Madden's promise to pay William Redd for renting the services of a slave named "Jeff" for one year.

		his		
Test	Willis	X	Madden	SEAL
Seth W. Redd		mark		

Loss of business and shortness of help were not the only problems facing the family now. Willis and Kitty had been proud when their daughter Sarah Ann was married to John Taylor, another free Negro from the neighborhood, in

1851—married by a registered minister, and the marriage recorded in the county courthouse. But not all of the Madden daughters had, in Willis Madden's eyes, behaved so admirably.

The youngest daughter, Maria, had taken up with a white man, and by the spring of 1859 she was pregnant with his child. Willis Madden wanted to send her over the mountains to live with relatives in the Shenandoah Valley, but Maria refused to go. She moved into a little cabin on the edge of Willis's land near the cemetery. No amount of arguing or pleading from her parents would make her break off with the man, and she was determined to stay on the farm to have her baby. Willis was deeply hurt and ashamed. He saw Maria's actions as an insult to the family—and to herself.

Maria Madden gave birth to a son, Thomas Obed, on January 26, 1860. He was my father.

There is a fragment of a letter in the Madden family papers, from Maria Madden to "Mr. Wilson Green" at "Culpeper Court House" (the county seat):

> . . . my father and mother have both sleighted me on your account. and if you cannot make it conveinat to come as soon as I wish you must send me a letter. no more at present so fare well
>
>   Maria Maden

The rest of the letter, now destroyed by age, remains in my memory. It stated that she was "in a family way" and detailed the tense situation between Maria and her parents. This would seem to suggest that Wilson Green might be the father of Thomas Obed Madden, Sr. However, stories that had circulation in the neighborhood rumored that Jack Wales, a slave trader from Stevensburg, was the father of Maria Madden's son. (T. O. Madden, Sr., always believed that his father was Jack Wales; two days before he died in

1949, he told his daughter Ruth, "You are not a Madden; you are a Wales.")

Maria's situation was a hard one for her parents to accept, but within a few months far greater tragedies began to enter Willis Madden's life.

The twin blows of Kitty Madden's death and the start of the Civil War fell within a year of each other. While the exact date of Kitty Madden's death is not recorded, she was alive during Maria Madden's first pregnancy (during the second half of 1859), as she is mentioned in Maria's letter to Wilson Green. But her name does not appear in the 1860 Census—taken in the summer of that year—indicating that she was dead by then. By the next spring—1861—Willis Madden, not yet recovered from the loss of his life's partner, saw the beginning of the war that was to engulf the countryside.

Soon the cracking of rifle fire and the thudding of artillery became a background to life in Culpeper County, the heavy guns rumbling like distant thunder—a storm that might break over Willis Madden's house at any time.

The travelers on the roads by Madden's tavern were replaced by soldiers and equipment trains. The same crossroads that had made Willis, and his tavern, grow and prosper now became his undoing. Because of these roads, the area around the tavern became a hotbed of military activity, and for much of the war it was right on the border between the Federal and Confederate lines. There were constant troop movements; Madden's tavern was still a landmark—but now to soldiers on the march. Willis Madden, from his yard or porch, could watch the men moving on toward the battlefields and see the wounded filtering back—from Cedar Mountain or Brandy Station or the dozens of smaller battles and skirmishes.

Still Willis's only son at home was Jack. Nat was living

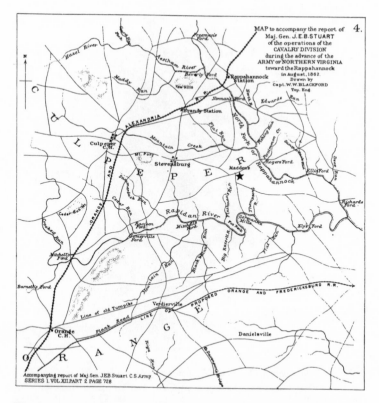

Wartime map of the Rapidan region. The Madden farm lay east of Stevensburg on the road from Culpeper—right in the eye of the storm that raged from 1861 to 1865. Six major battles and scores of small skirmishes were fought in a ring around the small homestead. Fired bullets excavated on the Madden farm testify to the hostile action that occurred within sight of the farmhouse.

at the county seat and for a time worked in the military hospital there. He was released from his duty in late 1861, perhaps because of illness, perhaps because he was needed to provide some help to his father. Certainly he came home at least for a while, because Willis placed his discharge with the other family papers:

The immortal Thomas ("Stonewall") Jackson, who commanded the Confederate forces at Cedar Mountain. Courtesy Cook Collection, Valentine Museum.

Camp Henry
Culpeper C.H.
Novr. 30th 1861

Nat Madden son of Willis is hereby released from service in the Hospital here, he being exempt by order of Lt. Col. Myler for reasons amply satisfactory

By order of
A.S. Taylor
Lt Col.   Geo. M. Williams

Of Willis's other children, French was living elsewhere in the county. Samuel and Margretta had settled in the North. Maria was still staying in her little cabin near the

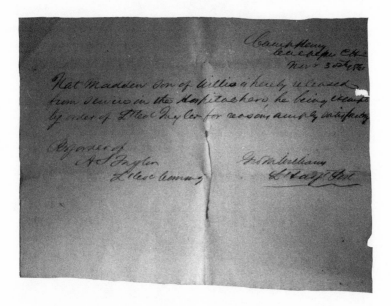

Nat Madden's release from duties in the Confederate hospital in Culpeper, Virginia, dated November 30, 1861.

family cemetery with her children (she had another son, my uncle, Willis Jackson Madden, in 1862).

The first Federal incursions into Culpeper County began in the summer of 1862. The Union occupied the county seat, and there were troop movements and skirmishes with Confederate forces in the general area of Madden's tavern, but the Yankees were finally driven back across the Rappahanock River into Fauquier County at the end of August, after the Battle of Cedar Mountain. There were strikes into Culpeper County all through the winter, but by the end of 1862 Madden's tavern remained safe—so far.

After looking over the farm he had worked so hard to buy and build up, Willis must have felt the sick fear of the helpless. The Confederate troops, short of supplies, scavenged everywhere they could. The Union armies were less gentle.

Battle of Cedar Mountain
August 9, 1862

The war was still in its infancy—barely a year old—when it burst upon the civilian population of the Culpeper area with the first of six major battles. Twelve miles due west of Madden's farm, Confederate General Stonewall Jackson battled the Union army of John Pope at Cedar Mountain.

They totally laid waste to an area, burning crops, killing livestock, tearing down buildings; they moved over the already scarred earth, taking what they needed, utterly destroying the rest. The Yankees had already destroyed much property in the center of the county during their stay. Willis knew what he could expect if the fighting or troops moved into his area with any force.

Even worse than the scavenging troops were the stragglers—men separated from their outfits and traveling by themselves. No one knew what to expect from stragglers. Some were only hungry, stopping to beg a little food. Others stopped at isolated farms—where the men had gone to war and only the women, children, and elderly were at home—and took advantage of the situations they found, committing acts of theft and destruction that could extend to assault and murder.

Willis was forbidden by law to own a weapon, but he knew that the law—if there still was a law—could no longer

Colt Army Model revolver found by the author in the attic of the farmhouse. This Federal sidearm was popular with troops of both sides. The weapon was likely obtained by Willis as protection against "stragglers." Photo, Stephen W. Sylvia.

protect him. Somehow, perhaps from a neighbor, perhaps from a soldier—either living or dead—he managed to acquire a revolver to protect himself and his family. If he ever had to use the gun, the fact has been hidden, like the bodies of stragglers.

From his farm Willis could hear the gunfire of scattered engagements and skirmishes through the winter and spring, into early 1863. In February he unwittingly entertained Major John Pelham, "the Gallant Pelham" of the Confederacy, who was on a reconnaissance mission. Major Heros von Borcke, who was with Pelham, gave a stereotyped account of the visit in his memoirs:

> We set off in the midst of a snowstorm, which increased in violence every hour. The snow ere long lay a foot deep, and the track of the road was soon so completely obliterated, that we stood in danger, in the midst of the vast wilderness and forest, which in this part of the country extends for many miles, of being lost altogether. At last, however, just as night was falling, we reached the house of a free negro, situated

about ten miles from our ultimate destination. Both ourselves and our horses were now about equally near exhaustion, and further progress being out of the question, we determined to seek shelter in this abode until the morning.

But the hospitality we had reckoned on was not granted so readily as we had anticipated. After gaining, through the open door, a glimpse of a comfortable interior lit up by the blaze of a huge wood fire, whose friendly warmth, even at that distance, seemed to reach our shivering limbs, what was our dismay at being suddenly shut out from this paradise, and having the door slammed in our faces, with the remark on the part of the black-faced proprietor of the mansion, that he would have "nothing to do with no stragglers."

Our disappointment was utter, for the position we were thus left in was, in fact, desperate, and for some minutes we stood wrapped in disconsolate silence. At last Pelham broke out: "This won't do at all; we can't possibly go on; to remain out of doors in this terrible weather is certain destruction, and as we are under the obligation of preserving our lives as long as possible, for the sake of our cause and country, I am going to fool this stupid old nigger, and play a trick off on him, which I think quite pardonable under the circumstances."

Having by repeated loud knocks induced the inhospitable negro to open the door, Pelham addressed him thus: "Mr. Madden" (this was the man's name) "you don't know what a good friend of yours I am, or what you are doing when you are about to treat us this way. That gentleman there" (pointing to me) "is the great General Lee himself; the other one is the French ambassador just arrived from Washington" (this alluded to Price, who being lately from Europe, and much better equipped than the rest, had a rather foreign appearance); "and I am a staff officer of the general's who is quite mad at being kept waiting outside so long after riding all this way on purpose to see you. In fact, if you let him stay any longer here in the cold, I'm afraid he'll shell your house as soon as his artillery comes up."

The old Negro was perfectly staggered by this long harangue, which was uttered with a perfectly serious countenance, that he immediately invited us in, with all matter of excuses for his mistake. Our horses were soon sheltered in the empty stable, and such a feed laid before them as they had not had for a long time, while we dried our garments before the blazing wood fire, our present sense of comfort being enhanced by anticipations of the future raised by the savory odors which reached us from the kitchen, where Mr. Madden was superintending in person the preparation of a repast suited to the distinguished rank of his guests.

Pelham was delighted at the success of his diplomatic ruse, and went on hoaxing the old negro in the same strain, until nothing could persuade him that all he had been told was not quite true; and though in the morning we endeavored to undeceive him, and paid him a liberal indemnity

Prussian soldier of fortune Major Heros von Borcke, left, served as J. E. B. Stuart's chief of staff. Major John Pelham, right, commander of J. E. B. Stuart's Horse Artillery, was a favorite of Robert E. Lee and had already achieved fame as a southern hero when he was killed at the Battle of Kelly's Ford in March 1863. Courtesy Cook Collection, Valentine Museum.

The greatest cavalry battle in the Western Hemisphere was fought on June 9, 1863, at Brandy Station, Virginia, seven miles from Madden's farm. There the legendary Confederate cavalry genius General J. E. B. Stuart defeated the Union troops of General Alfred Pleasonton in a daylong clash.

for the stratagem, he continued to inflate himself with a sense of his own importance at having been honored with a visit from such distinguished guests.

It was a brief incident, a joke played by a soldier who took delight in having fooled a "stupid old nigger." A month later John Pelham, young trickster and seasoned soldier, died in a cavalry charge at Kelly's Ford at age twenty-four.

Willis Madden's agony was to be more enduring. The war moved ever closer. There were more troop movements and skirmishes in the vicinity into April, but Willis's property escaped damage. On April 23, 1863, a sharp skirmish broke out between Confederates and Yankees up from Germanna Ford (much of northern Orange County, along the Rapidan, was in Federal hands). The fighting was almost within sight of the tavern, and Willis would have heard the guns and the battle cries. Soon there were more Federal

The dashing Rebel cavalryman James Ewell Brown Stuart as he looked at the time of the Battle of Brandy Station. Cook Collection, Valentine Museum.

incursions; fighting intensified. Spent bullets found in the fields around Madden's tavern tell of skirmishes that Willis must have seen from his own house. On June 9, 1863, the Battle of Brandy Station began; still known as the largest cavalry battle the Western world has known, the fighting raged only a few miles from Willis's farm.

More Federal troops crossed into Culpeper, some detachments passing within a stone's throw of the tavern. For the

General George G. Meade's huge army camped for miles around the Culpeper area, taking over farms and residences at will. This image was taken at Meade's headquarters in Culpeper in 1863.

rest of the year the territory under each army's control was constantly changing, but by late 1863 the eastern portion of the county was firmly under Federal occupation. General Grant himself was at the county seat. More than one hundred thousand men were camped in Culpeper County over the winter and into the spring, many of them near Stevensburg.

The Federal troops finally left the county for good—except for a few scattered raids—the following May. But by then it was too late for Willis Madden. His farm had survived untouched until the last six months of the Federal presence, but then there were thousands of men in the area, camped for the winter, idle, scavenging for extra supplies or for the sake of the damage they could do. And all the things that Willis had feared began to happen.

Throughout that terrible fall and winter and spring of 1863–1864, Willis Madden was forced to play host to suc-

Approximately three hundred thousand Federal and Confederate troops camped in Orange and Culpeper counties in the winter of 1863–1864. Their eight-month stay ravaged the countryside and rendered many families destitute.

cessive groups of Union soldiers. They descended on the farm like a cloud of locusts. Each group would seem to pick the place clean and move on—and then the next troops would somehow find still more to take. Willis's horses and his cart were stolen. Doors of farm buildings were broken down, and supplies and equipment taken or ruined. The livestock were driven off or slaughtered—eaten by the soldiers or just left to rot where they fell. Finally even the outbuildings and fences were destroyed, and the entire woodlot of three acres was cut down, the pieces taken away and used for firewood and timbers for the soldiers' shelters. When the soldiers left, they took or destroyed what was left of the food and fodder. They left the house standing—and Willis Madden, at age sixty-five, with his farm stripped of almost everything of value.

It was one of the cruel ironies of the war. Willis Madden had never been a slave, but he was a member of the Negro

Scars from the Civil War are still visible in the Virginia countryside. These cannon emplacements overlooking the Rapidan River near Montpelier were constructed by Robert E. Lee's troops in the fall of 1863. Courtesy Moss Publications.

race. And he was ruined by the very army that was supposedly fighting to bring freedom and justice to that race. For Willis Madden, there was no justice. He survived, but he was never the same again. He hung on, eating the few supplies that he had managed to hide from the troops and what he could gather and trap, somehow finding seed to plant, rounding up the livestock that had not been killed or carried off by the foraging troops. The credit that he had before the war had turned into debts that he could not pay. The memory of all he had lost gnawed at him. Brooding over his shattered life, Willis started to slip into a state of depression from which he never completely recovered.

Chapter Seven

THE LAST YEARS

The Five Parts of Culpeper County—

First, the Piney Woods, abounding in flint rock, chinquepins and brandy. It also has some very fine water, not extensively used, however, unless a frost happens to blight the apple blossoms. . . . The great rendezvous . . . is Griffinsburg, or the Box as it is sometimes called, where they vote and fight audaciously, for they are a pugnacious sort.

Second, the Little Fork, celebrated for associations, camp meetings, and much in the way of watermelons. The people here meet at the store of "old Mac" [at Jeffersonton], whittle sticks and tell monstrous yarns about fox hunting. Being generally under camp meeting influence they differ from the dwellers in the "pines" in not being much addicted to fighting.

Third, the Chinquepin Neck, not remarkable for much besides Willis Madden's and voting the Democratic ticket. It once had a fragment of plank road, which was to have rejuvenated old Fredericksburg, (but didn't) and a bridge at Germanna.

Fourth, the Flat Grounds a piece of level land, so wet in winter, that the Rev. Mr. Pollock once said, he believed it never leaked, and so dry in summer that you can't drive a nail into it without greasing. This division has Mitchell's Station for its capital, which in winter may be called a seaport from the quantity of water surrounding it, and its heavy and increasing trade in liquor and railroad ties.

Lead bullets, brass buttons, and miscellaneous articles of military gear found on the Madden farm attest to its wartime occupants. This is but a sampling of the artifacts recovered over the years by family members and relic hunters. Photo, Stephen W. Sylvia.

Fifth, the Court House or Red Land Division, noted for the Freedmen's Bureau, Antioch Church, and the Town of Fairfax, which is said to have a town Sergeant, a board of trustees, and many conveniences for drinking. It has also trap rocks, red mud, much sumac, and great quantities of sassafras. There is a great variety of soil, and much diversity of people, the mass of whom are conservative. We have but little scallawag, less carpetbag, but considerable loil league, which has a respectable, but misled colored man for president, and a brick-laying carpetbagger for secretary.

Culpeper Observer, *September 7, 1868*

When the war finally ended, Willis was nearly broke. The man who once had hundreds of dollars of credit in Fredericksburg did not have the money to pay a tax bill of less than a dollar. In 1868 and 1870 he was in arrears on taxes of less than seventy cents a year. He had *no* cash on hand. In the years after the war Willis Madden, like many others, lived by what he could raise or make on the farm. The house and yard, once so neatly kept, became shabby. Weeds grew in the old wagonyard. Weatherboards had loosened from the house, which had not seen a coat of whitewash for years.

Slowly Willis began to rebuild his farm and his family. His sons French, Nat, and Jack visited and helped when they could, and William Hackley was again working on the place. Maria and her boys came home at last to live with Willis. His granddaughter Margaret Taylor, Sarah Ann's daughter, also came to live with her grandfather. Willis had a household again.

There were visits and letters to and from Samuel and Margretta, and their families, living in Washington, D.C. Samuel was by now a well-known preacher among the Negroes in Virginia, Washington, D.C., and Maryland. He had moved to Washington from Baltimore during the war and had settled there. In late 1864 he had applied for and been appointed to the position of chaplain of the Freedmen's Hospital in Washington, by order of President Abraham Lincoln, but the news had not reached Willis until the war was over:

[To] Abraham Lincoln
President of the United States

Honorable Sir

       Being anxious to accomplish the greatest amount of good to the colored soldiers of the United States Army I must respectfully ask to be appointed Hospital Chaplain at the Hospital for colored troops & Freedmen in Washington, D.C.

Washington, D.C.

August 1864   Your obedient servant
             Samuel W. Madden

In August 1864 Willis's son Samuel wrote a letter, top, to President Lincoln requesting posting as "Chaplain at the Hospital for the colored troops & Freedmen in Washington, D.C." Samuel Madden's presidential appointment, bottom, to the post of chaplain to the Freedman's Hospital in Washington, D.C.

Executive Mansion
Washington 19 November 1864

[To] The Secretary of War
Sir

The President requested that an appointment be issued to Rev. S. W. Madden of Virginia (Colored) for the position of Hospital Chaplain at the Freedmens' Hospital, Washington, D.C.

Your Obt. Servant
John Hay

Letters to Willis Madden from his son Samuel and daughter-in-law, in 1868, are preserved among the Madden family papers. Both letters were written on the same sheet of paper to save writing paper and postage. Samuel's wife was intent on matching Willis with one of several women whom she knew. Samuel seems to have been more concerned with getting one of the hogs that Willis was planning to slaughter for meat:

Alexandria, Va. Nov. 18, 1868

Dear Father:

Your letter was received last week we were glad to hear that you and the family were well. The baby and myself are not very well he has the chills, and I am suffering with a cold. My wife is tolerably well.

We are pleased to learn that your hogs are fine, and that your corn crop is good so you can see that the Lord is kind to the poor. You can send our hog when you kill or bring it down when you come, let us know what day you will come and I will meet you or have some one meet you.

I will have to go down the country on next Wednesday if I am well enough and if my family is well and if the Lord will, and get home on the second of Dece.—But my wife will be at home if you have made your arrangements to come before the 2nd come on my wife will take care of you. But

write and let us know when to expect you, and when to look
for the hog. Please send or bring me
1 Gallon dried Beans and
1 Gallon dried peas, and I will pay you for them.
Give my love to all and accept the same for yourself.

As ever your son
S. W. Madden

[Written on reverse]

Alexandria Va.
Nov. 19, 1868

Dear Grandfather,

I persuaded Sammy to keep this leter a few hour longer
than I might write a line to you. We have heard so little from
you since our return from the country that we feared you
were sick as well as ourselves, but were glad to know that
the delay in the mails was the principal cause of your silence.

We were very glad to know that you are caring to make
us a visit—we wil strive to make it pleasant for you. Come
when you are ready and see our little city—I guess it has
changed in many respects since you saw it last.

I will take you to see the lady I wrote you of last summer—perhaps you may be able to make a conquest of her,
but if you should fail, why I have another in view who is
away at present.

Give my love to Sister Maria and family, also to the
children, especially little Margaret. I hope that she is learning to housekeep nicely for you.

Willis is fretting so that I cannot write more.

Affectionately yours,
M. A. Madden

A later letter is from Margretta, who was then living in
Georgetown, near Washington, D.C.:

George Town Feb. 25th 1875

Dear Father

I recieved your last letter and was sorry to hear that you
was all sick, and hope that by this time you are all in your

usual health. After I got home, I was thinking the matter over, I thought, as the times was hard, and the winter seemed to be cold and hard also I had better stay here, and I could get a little chance of earning a little, and as you had no logs on your place, and it would put you to trouble to fix the place up, I had better stay here, this winter[.] I sent you a letter, right-back, in answer to the other one, telling you not to fix up, but I expect you did not get that letter as you mentioned it in your last, and as long as you have fixed it up, you had better rent it, as it might help you along, as my health is not very good, I have a bad cough, and can't do much hard work as I used to do and can't expose myself, and if you get any rent from the huse, you had better settle to William Hackley for helping to fix it[.] we have a remarkable hard & cold winter, one could hardly keep warm, no work of any account to do, a good deal of sickness and great many deaths, but we are all looking forward to an early Spring that will help to make things look brighter[.] Anna is very well, her health is good, she goes to school, and gets on very nicely, she sends her Loves and kisses to her grandfather[.] Give my love to Marie, and all my inquiring Friends
I send my Love to you
no more at present
But remain your affectionate Daughter
    Margretta Madden
I would like you to answer this soon, Direct as formerly
                                    M. M.

The members of the family in Culpeper were also making contributions toward the educational and spiritual life of the community. In 1866 Jack and Maria received Bibles and hymnals from the Freedmen's Bureau, the federal agency set up to oversee the situation of newly freed slaves. They organized a school—teaching Bible classes in addition to elementary school—at the county seat.

Maria was also organizing a small school at Madden's tavern; she had hired a Mr. Lucas, an Englishman living in the

Application of _____ **for**

Stores taken and used by the U. S. Army.

State of *Virginia*
County of *Culpeper* } ss.

I, *Willis Madden*
aged *sixty six* years, on my oath, state that I am a CITIZEN and ACTUAL
RESIDENT of the County of *Culpeper* and State of *Virginia*
and that I was such at the time my claim hereinafter set forth originated; and that I was, at the date
my said claim originated, and have been ever since, loyal to the Government of the United States—
that on or about the *first* day of *August* in the year one
thousand eight hundred and sixty *two* at or near the _____ of
_____ in the County of *Culpeper* in the State of
Virginia the following *Naked* Stores
were taken from me by *Troops under command*
of Genl Patrick.

to wit: 2 Horses valued at 100—1 Horse cart 20/	170	00
4 Bushels Corn (Shelled) ⅔ Pk 200 lbs Bacon lb	40	00
2 Iron Tools & (of Hay, 2 Steel)	46	00
About the 1st of May 1863 by Troops of Genl Stoneman		
to wit: 2 Horses valued at 150 repair 35 Bush Corn(Shelled) 5th	312	50
35 lbs Bacon lb & 4 Iron Tools 5/ each	4	65
In September 1863 by Cavalry Pickets (42)		
5 Large Hogs (valued) at	45	00
In December by Troops of the army of the Potomac		
7 Head of Cattle (valued at)	100	00
150 Bushels Corn (Shelled) 5th	75	00
Amt Carried (over)	793	15

under the following circumstances:

X

area, to teach her sons to read and write.* By 1868 there
was a formal school at the old tavern, set up by the Freedmen's Bureau. The teacher was a Mr. M. L. Tabb, who
boarded with Willis Madden for ten dollars a month.

Willis also helped found the Ebenezer Baptist Church,
built on his land in 1867. Maria named the church ("Ebenezer" was interpreted as "Thus far hath the Lord brought
us"), and Samuel, French, and Nat came home for the dedication. This original church, which contained a school-
room, lasted until 1884, when it burned. The present
Ebenezer Church was completed in 1886, and it stands across
the road from the site of the first one.

The Ebenezer congregation consisted of a few older, free
Negroes and several newly freed slaves; the original members of the church, besides Willis and Maria, were Jack Davis
(who became the first minister), Robert Webb, Henry Gil-
lison, Elizabeth Taylor (perhaps one of Willis's grand-
daughters), and Thomas Fields. My father was one of the
only members of the congregation who could read and write.
He became the clerk at the tender age of seven, keeping the
minutes from the trustees' meetings and reading the Bible
at services.

Maria Madden was married in 1868 to Thomas Fields, a
fellow member of the Ebenezer congregation, and they lived
on the farm near Willis. After Thomas Fields's early death
in 1870, Maria and her boys returned to Willis's house. By
then the household also included Nancy Hurley, another
young Madden relative who later married one of the Bundys.

Except for Maria, most of Willis's children had now left
or would soon leave the county. Nathaniel Madden moved

*Thomas Obed Madden always referred to his teacher formally, merely as
Mr. Lucas. He was apparently a neighbor, H. Rollin Lucas, later one of the
witnesses to Willis Madden's will; the 1880 Culpeper County Census lists his
birthplace as England.

to Pittsburgh, Pennsylvania, just before 1870. Willis sold his son Jack a parcel of the tavern tract in 1874, around the time of Jack's marriage to Cornelia Washington. But within a few years Jack had moved to Altoona, Pennsylvania.

Willis Madden, old Willis now, was still a poor farmer. Not until 1871 had he been able to file a claim for the Civil War troop damage that had nearly wiped him out. With Samuel's help, he made his application, and since he hadn't borne arms against the Federal government, his claim was processed. But of the $2,441.15 appraisal for his stolen and destroyed property, he was awarded only $879, barely a third of the value:

Willis Madden's Civil War Claims.   Date: April 14, 1871

Name: Willis Madden
Residence: Stephensburg, Va. (Culpeper Co.)
Subject-Matter: Horses, cart, forage, bacon, farmproduce, fodder, wood, taken in Virginia.
Amount claimed: $2441 15 / 00   Amount Allowed: $879
Cochran & Lewis, Attorneys, Culpeper
Dec. 9, 1872. Reported to Congress—
Allowed $879 by Private Act of Mch. 3d 1873 and filed with 3d Auditor

Culpeper State of Va.
We the undersigned citizen freeholders of the County and State aforesaid have been called upon to estimate & value the timber (including fencing) wood etc. consumed by Troops of the Federal Army under the [torn] Col. Brooke commanding the 1st [torn] 2nd Corps Major General Hancock commanding [torn] during the winter of 1863 1864 when [torn] was occupied by the Army of the Potomac under the command Lieut. General [torn] upon the premises of Willis Madden (a man of colour) whose farm lies upon both the main road leading from Culpeper to Fredericksburg. After having carefully examined measured and estimated the quality of fencing material consumed by the said [Troops?] upon the premises of the said Willis Madden upon our oaths make the following estimate and valuation

120

To three acres of woodland at 20 cords per acre—60 cords at $4 per cord	$240
To 9000 rails at $25 per thousand	475
To one house destroyed	100
	$815

George W. Stone
W. A. Coleman
John Turner

The money did pay Willis's debts and let him make some repairs to the now dilapidated house, but he was too old, and too tired, to try to build things up completely again. The old days of Madden's tavern and prosperity were gone forever for him, and he knew it.

While the money made things a little easier for Willis, it also created some problems within the family. My father remembered the uneasy relationship between Maria and her brother Samuel. Samuel, the minister, looked down on his sister for having borne two illegitimate children. And after Samuel helped press Willis Madden's claim for war damages, a portion of this money went to Samuel. Maria resented Samuel's attitude toward her and her sons and believed that he got more than his share of the money—money she thought should have gone to Willis Madden and the family members sharing his household.

Willis was now in his middle seventies. He spent his days tending his garden, doing what farm chores he still could, and taking walks around the farm. Soon the depression that had plagued him since the end of the war deepened. He gradually slipped away as he approached eighty, just sitting in the sun or a warm corner, his mind drifting back over the old days, the times long gone at Madden's tavern. He saw in his family and visitors the faces of friends and relatives long dead: Kitty and their babies, old Sarah, his sisters

. . . and his own young self—healthy, prosperous, respected
. . . Mr. Willis Madden.

The end came on the first day of December 1879. Willis Madden was buried in the oak grove beside Kitty and Sarah. His will, probated in Culpeper the following April, stated that he was "at enmity with no man."

His personal property was valued at a total of $66.25. His clock was appraised at $3. Nearly half of the remaining value was assigned to two cows and a plow. A few items of furniture—three beds, two bureaus, and a table and chairs—completed the listing.

Samuel was the executor of the estate. Maria inherited the house and eleven acres. In 1883 she bought the remaining portion of the farm. The land, in the deed description, was "bounded by . . . the Fredericksburg Road . . . the Peoli Road . . . the Stevensburg Road . . ."—the old main thoroughfares that had been responsible for the rise of Madden's tavern. They were fast becoming little more than backcountry roads.

A year after Willis Madden's death the following appeared in a Culpeper newspaper. It could well have served as his epitaph:

> Before the War, the tavern in the lower end of the county, kept by Willis Madden, a colored man, was patronized by all persons who happened to be traveling that way. It was about the only place between Culpeper and Fredericksburg where accommodations for man or horse could be found. We stopped there once in September 1860, to get dinner and at the table we found Aleck Marshall, of Fauqier, John L. Marye, Jr., of Fredericksburg, Dr. Boulware of Caroline, and James O. Harris, Dr. Sandy Gordon, and William Massey Simms of Culpeper. "Uncle Willis," as everybody called him, was a highly respectable man and his establishment

was deservedly popular. It was one of the institutions of the day. We believe the War broke it up.

Ellis B. Williams, editor,
Culpeper Exponent, December 10, 1880

Chapter Eight

THOMAS OBED

and

LANDONIA STOKES MADDEN

ᴀᴓᴓᴀ

Cicero's Six Mistakes That Man Makes:
1. *The decision that legal advancement is made by crushing others.*
2. *To worry about things that can't be changed or corrected.*
3. *Insisting that things are impossible and we can't accomplish them.*
4. *Refusal to set aside trivial purposes.*
5. *Neglecting development and refinement of the mind and not acquiring the habit of reading and studying.*
6. *Attempting to compel others to believe and live as we do.*

Some favorite mottoes of T. O. Madden, Sr.

The end of the last chapter is also the end of the things that I know only through family stories and documents. My ancestors were the heroes of the family tales that I heard as a boy: Sarah Madden, who kept her family together against the odds; Willis Madden, "a man among men," as I can still hear my father saying. I grew up in awe of these mighty figures, the stuff of myth and legend in my boy-hood dreams. But I never knew them in real life.

Beginning with this chapter, my family's more recent history is told. I either personally knew the people involved who recounted their stories to me—I heard about my parents' early lives from my parents or from my older brothers and sisters, who were there when these things happened—or I remember these things myself.

I have relied especially on my sister Ruth to help fill in things that happened before I was born and when I was very young. Ruth, whose memory is incredible, is now ninety-eight, eleven years older than I am. She can clearly remember things back to the late 1890s.

My father, Thomas Obed Madden, spent his earliest years on his grandfather Willis Madden's farm. The farm had come to be called Madden's, or Maddenville, when Willis Madden was still operating his tavern. This happened with many taverns, whose many outbuildings gave them the look of small villages. After the tavern had gone out of business, my family kept the name Maddenville for the farm. The name remains to this day.

My grandmother Maria Madden, had hired an Englishman, Mr. Lucas, to teach her sons—my father, Thomas Obed Madden, and my uncle, Willis Jackson Madden—to read and write. For the rest of his life Daddy remembered Mr. Lucas, and the very proper way he spoke and taught his pupils to speak. My father and his brother were about the only Negroes in the neighborhood who were literate in the early years after the Civil War.

When he was ten, my father went to Pittsburgh, Pennsylvania, where he lived with his uncle Nat (Nathaniel) Madden and his family. The Pittsburgh Maddens were devout Presbyterians, and they decided to make my father into a missionary. They sent him to school there, with the idea that he would be trained to become a missionary to

Liberia. He was in school there for more than four years, but he was not as enthusiastic about becoming a missionary as his uncle was to make him one. So, when he was fourteen, my father quit school and went to work as a barber in Pittsburgh.

Before integration there were colored barbershops and there were white barbershops, but most barbers—the best barbers anyway, I think—were colored. After integration the health department came into the picture and regulations were passed. You had to go to school to learn barbering, there got to be money in it, and then the white people took it up. But barbering was still a dirty job in my father's youth. He tried to be a barber, but he didn't like it.

He started out as a barber's apprentice. An apprentice had to lather up the customer; then the barber came and shaved him. When the barber was through, the apprentice had to wipe off the customer and wash him. People would come in after a fight or after they had gotten hurt, and the apprentice put leeches on them to suck down bruises. The apprentices also had to shine shoes. All this made my father feel like a servant, and he did not want to be a servant. He hated the idea of waiting on anybody, doing what he called "servant's work."

Five years after he had come to Pittsburgh, when my father was about fifteen, his mother, Maria Madden, became ill, and Willis Madden began to get feeble. My father used that as an excuse to return home to Culpeper County and Maddenville.

It was after returning to Maddenville that my father found his profession. He tutored two of his neighbors, both Negroes: Lawrence Phillips, who worked in a sawmill, and Henry Burrell, who worked on Ab Willis's farm. He taught them to read and write, and they both received better-paying positions because they were able to do so. A little while after that both went to Washington and got jobs with the federal government—jobs that gave them good livings.

Daddy stayed in Culpeper County, working as a barber to support himself. He was just making ends meet, but he had a goal: He was going to be a teacher.

In addition to working as a barber, my father attended the Summer Institute for Teachers (also called the Summer Normal School), which was held in the town of Culpeper. The county sponsored the Summer Institute; it was a special six-week course to enable Negroes to get teaching certificates. Even after he had become a teacher, Daddy still attended these classes to sharpen his skills and keep up with new developments.

At the 1889 Summer Institute he met Landonia Randolph Stokes, a native of Prince William County. Landonia Stokes was then a teacher at Manassas; she, too, was attending the Summer Institute to further her education. During the six weeks that she was in Culpeper she roomed with Mr. and Mrs. Walter West, schoolteachers who lived in the town. And in those six weeks she found that she had much in common with Thomas Obed Madden. After a courtship of a little less than a year, they were married at her family home in Wellington, near Manassas, on April 23, 1890. The new Mrs. Madden came home with her husband to Maddenville farm, and they both taught in the segregated county schools.

My mother's father, Francis Stokes, who was so light-skinned that many said he was a white man, had been a wagoneer for the Confederate Army in the Civil War. He served from the Battle of Manassas right through to the end of the war. In civilian life he was a skilled wheelwright, carpenter, and cabinetmaker. He died in June 1890, right after my parents were married. Her mother, Sally Pinn Stokes—Grandma Stokes—lived until 1923, long enough that all her Madden grandchildren remembered her. Our father's mother, Maria Madden Fields, died before any of her grandchildren were born, and Grandma Stokes was the only grandparent we knew. Mama would take all her children home at least once a year for a big family gathering at the Stokes farm, with Grandma and our uncles and aunts and cousins.

My parents lived in the old tavern at Maddenville. My father's dream was to build a new house of his own, but there was never enough money. Finally he settled for renovating the old place and building an addition, which he did from 1900 to 1905. Besides the addition, the loft of the old tavern was plastered, covering the bare rafters and sheathing boards that had been exposed since Willis Madden's time. Dormers were added to the roof, making more space and light in the rooms up under the eaves.

The additions were needed; the old house was getting crowded. My parents were raising a large family. A year after their marriage, April 16, 1891, my father hitched our mare Maybelle up to the dogcart and went after old lady Bundy, the local midwife. He was disappointed that his firstborn was a girl—in fact, his first four children were girls—but finally he got his boys, too.

There were twelve of us, six girls and six boys: Odenla, or Denny (born April 16, 1891); Ruth Columbia (May 1, 1892); Sarah Maria, or Sally (November 9, 1893); Gladys (January 1, 1895; she died young, of diphtheria); Oliver Wendell, or O.W. (February 2, 1896); Melissa Mason (May 22, 1897); Edward Everett, or Ev (October 11, 1898); Ralph (born and died in June 1899), Hannibal Hamlin (January 20, 1902); Thomas Obed, Jr.—myself, T.O. (July 11, 1903); Nathaniel, or Nat (April 15, 1906); and Landonia (May 31, 1909).

It was hard life, but in many ways a good one. My father believed in cold baths every morning, and we all had to work on the farm as soon as we were able; but our parents also saw to it that we were educated. We missed a lot of school time since we had to help on the farm, but my father tutored the older children in the evenings, and later my mother did the same for the younger ones. Our primer was

Longfellow, and later there were other classics. My parents had Bible readings and prayers morning and evening, and before bedtime we sang hymns and closed with the Lord's Prayer.

We were poor, but we did have magazines and books. My father's cousins Edith and Gertrude, daughters of Samuel Madden, were teachers and librarians in Washington, D.C., and regularly sent us discarded books—not just one or two but a whole carton of books and magazines at a time. My father read them first, and then he made us read them. The newspaper came out once a week, and Daddy always sat and read it to us.

Mama sewed some of our clothes, and with so many children in the family, we wore a lot of hand-me-downs. But just as our Madden cousins sent us books, so Grandma Stokes and our aunt Kate Stokes sent us secondhand clothes and shoes, and Mama made these over for us.

Mama's sister-in-law Kate Stokes, who was married to Uncle Travis, was an Irishwoman, and they lived in New York. She used to send barrels of clothes—beautiful clothes. Aunt Kate had seen all my mother's children at the family reunion at Manassas, and she remembered us.

I don't know what Aunt Kate did in New York, but Mama could look for a barrel of expensive dresses to come down every year, and she would rip those dresses up and make clothes for us. And there were always some shoes; they were men's shoes, but we all wore them, even the girls.

Grandma Stokes sent clothes down in fall, by train, but on the day they came we couldn't open the box until all the chores were done. We would be sniffing around and peeking in the cracks, but that box wasn't opened until after we had done our work—milked the cows, carried in water and firewood, had breakfast, and washed the dishes. Then the box was opened. Besides clothes, Grandma had a little something else in there for us. Every year she sent gifts to her grandchildren—not fancy presents, perhaps, but little things to show that she loved us and was thinking of us. My sister Ruth still has a plate on her wall that Grandma Stokes sent her before she was five years old. She sent each one of her grandchildren a plate that year.

My mother taught at the Maddenville school near home, my father at the Lignum school a few miles down the road. School opened the first day of October and ended the last day of February, five months, running in the time when the children were less needed for farm work. At first each of them was paid $26 a month for the five-month term—a total of $130 each. Later my father's salary was raised to $30 a month, or $150 for the term because he had a little bit better grade in certificate. Even with this raise, my parents' combined yearly salaries were less than $300.

The contracts required that they had to keep the schools open and to keep the buildings clean, sweep the floor, and have the fire in the schoolhouse stove made for the children, in addition to teaching. Some teachers did all this work themselves, but my father, always refusing to do "servant's work," assigned several students every day to do the cleaning and tend the fire. My mother's contract for 1892 is typical:

THIS ARTICLE OF AGREEMENT, between THE BOARD OF SCHOOL TRUSTEES of Stevensburg School District of Culpeper County, of the one part, and L. R. Madden, of the other part:

WITNESSETH, That the said L. R. Madden, under the supervision and direction of the said Board, but subject, nevertheless, to the visitation and lawful authority of the County Superintendent, agrees to teach in No. B schoolhouse for the term of five months at a compensation of $26.00 per month, for a lawful school, with a lawful average daily attendance of pupils: provided, however, that an average of less than ten will not be recognized nor paid for, and that any failure on the part of the said teacher to report correctly

The author's mother, Landonia Madden, and her students ca. 1900.

the daily average, as required, to the Superintendent, shall vitiate this contract—the said amount to be paid when collected, the Board reserving the right to dismiss the said L. R. Madden at any time, for cause, paying her for her services in accordance with this agreement to the date of her dismissal.

It is also agreed that the said L. R. Madden shall keep the prescribed school register, (to be furnished by the Clerk of the Board of School Trustees), open school at 9 o'clock in the morning, give 30 minutes at 12 o'clock, and close the school at 3:30 o'clock in the evening, (a school day shall consist of 6 hours and 30 minutes, and a school month of four weeks of five school days each); obey all school laws and regulations, make monthly and term reports to the County Superintendent, according to the forms furnished, and return the school register to the Clerk of the Board of Trustees at the end of the term in good order. For the loss or abuse of the school register, or any failure to make a monthly or term report to the County Superintendent within three days after the expiration of the month or term, the said L. R. Madden shall be subject to a fine, at the discretion of the Board, of not more than five dollars. The fine, in all cases, shall be retained out of the teacher's pay, and to go into the funds of the district for the pay of teachers.

It is further agreed that the fire shall be made, or caused to be made, and the floor shall regularly be swept, or caused to be swept by the said L. R. Madden, the Board providing the fuel, brooms and brushes therefor; and that that actual possession of the school-house shall be considered by both parties as remaining and being at all times in the said Board or their successors.

In 1901 my mother stopped teaching. The school trustees thought that two salaries—a grand total of $56 per month—was too much money coming to one Negro family. The community wouldn't stand up for my parents. Enough of the neighbors also felt this way: that two teachers' salaries coming into the Madden family at one time were just too much.

My mother didn't try to find another teaching job because as more children came, it had become harder to take care of the younger ones when my parents were away. Taking care of the children had been getting more difficult for several years. Mama didn't teach in late 1898, after Everett was born. She went back to the classroom the next year, but she stopped teaching for good when Everett was three years old. At the time my mother stopped teaching, she already had eight children, with six living. She was expecting Hannibal, her ninth baby. At this time my father left the Lignum school and took her place as teacher at the Maddenville school.

Until near the time Everett was born, when my mother and father both worked, old William Hackley—in his seventies and called Uncle William by then—still helped around the farm and served as the baby-sitter for my brothers and sisters who were too young to go to school. After Everett was born, when Uncle William was getting too old for baby-

Thomas Obed Madden, Sr., Landonia, and nine of their twelve children. Taken about 1906 when T. O., Jr., was three years old. He is leaning against his father's knee.

sitting, Grandma Stokes sent a neighbor, a girl named Frances Page, down from Manassas. But Frances didn't work out. One day she just left Everett alone and went off visiting. Daddy and Mama put her on the train back to Manassas the next day. After Frances Page left, Uncle William Hackley took care of Everett for a while, until Ev became too much of a handful for the old man. He finally ordered Uncle William, "I want a piece of bread with butter on it, YOU HEAR ME!" and Uncle William wouldn't take that from a child, so he stopped baby-sitting. After that Mama made Ruth and Denny stay at the house to watch Everett. Each girl took baby-sitting duty in the morning one day and the evening the next. By switching off, Ruth and Denny would be able to finish out that year at school. But after several months of this Mama decided it was better for her to stop teaching and stay home and do for herself, and we never had another baby-sitter.

William Hackley worked on the farm and helped look after the children almost until his death in the early 1900s. Although he lived at Maddenville for nearly a half century, none of us who are still living knows exactly how he fitted into the Madden family, only that he was said to be a blood relation. Even my sister Ruth, who knew William Hackley, knows only that he was a relative. He was working for Willis Madden in 1850, and from his age, given as thirty in the census in that year, he was born about 1820. He may have been Willis Madden's nephew since he was the right age to be a son of Willis Madden's sister Fanny Madden Hackley.

As he neared his end, Uncle William asked my father to take care of him in his old age, but Daddy didn't know if he could take care of himself and his own family, much less Uncle William, and he wouldn't agree. Things were never quite the same between my parents and Uncle William after that. Uncle William had spent most of his life on the farm, he had worked for Willis Madden, and he had helped my grandmother and now my parents. He must have felt that my parents owed him his retirement, but they barely had enough money to support their own children.

My sister Ruth remembers William Hackley in the happy time when he was still the family baby-sitter. The children knew him as Uncle Willie Hackley, or sometimes Hackie-Willie. His house, a little log house surrounded by the smoothest, greenest grass, was a special place for the children. Besides the regular baby-sitting days, my older brothers and sisters looked forward to going down there on Sundays for visits. His house had a wooden ladder to the loft, which was a place of mystery. He let the children sit on the ladder, but he never let them stick their heads into that loft, where he slept. Sometimes they would inch up the steps toward the loft, but he always caught them before they reached the top; just before they were able to peek into the loft, they'd hear him calling, "Come down, come down." He cooked the old way, in the fireplace; he never had anything but a fireplace, but he made the best-tasting bread that you ever put in your mouth. He always gave "his" children horehound candy when they got ready to leave.

My mother didn't known anything about farming when she got married, but she learned. She had to harrow the fields because we couldn't get anyone else to do this. Daddy did the plowing until his boys got old enough. Mama also raised chickens and sold the eggs.

After my mother stopped teaching, she looked after the farm and expanded her chicken flock to get more eggs to sell, to replace the salary that she had lost. She also took in boarders, teachers from the Summer Institutes. Julia Mason, who taught the course at which my parents met, often stayed with us.

Besides chickens, my mother raised turkeys. Turkey farming was the lifeline for some families, including ours. Women would follow the turkeys and chicks as if they were children. They followed them around during the day to watch over them while they ranged and herded them back to their coops at night and if it stormed. Turkeys were sold only for the Thanksgiving and Christmas markets; each turkey brought five to ten dollars. This was tremendous money for my parents at a time when my father was earning thirty dollars a month teaching.

Another reason my mother never tried to go back to teaching was that people were stealing from us, and someone needed to stay close to home to watch the place. After my father had put corn in the horses' manger at night, someone was coming up the back way and taking it out. Some of the neighbors were stealing chickens and eggs from our henhouse, too. We also had hay stored in an old abandoned house—what we called the glebe house, near the old church site—and somebody was coming in and stealing that. Daddy had to stop it, so he hid in the old house to catch the thief. He was waiting there when the thief came and stuck his head in the hole where there had been a stovepipe. My father got excited and coughed, and whoever was out there knew he had better not come in to get that hay, because Daddy might have a shotgun with him. He did. My father began to tell the neighbors the name of the man he thought had been stealing the hay, and the man came up to the house after him. Daddy was ready to go out to meet him—with his shotgun—but Grandma Stokes was visiting, and she kept him from going out.

My father's first two students had gone away to Washington and gotten jobs that paid much more money than my father made as a teacher, but one of my parents' later students actually put my father out of his job.

There were two young ladies whom both my mother and my father had taught. One was Lillie Fields, and the other was Mable Carter. After school in Culpeper County they had gone to Virginia Normal Institute in Petersburg for four years. They returned to the county and applied for teaching positions. Lillie Fields's father worked for Ab Willis, who owned Sherwood farm—hundreds of acres of prime land a little to the south of Maddenville—as well as the general store at the nearby village of Lignum. Mable Carter's father worked for Johnny Payne, who owned a big sawmill in the neighborhood. The fathers asked their employers, who had quite a bit of clout with the county supervisors, to put in a good word for the girls and help them get the positions they wanted. Mable Carter wanted to teach near her home, near Maddenville.

Daddy had taken over the Maddenville school seven years before, when Mama had stopped teaching. It suited him, being just across the road, within walking distance of our farm. He was close to home and to his family.

The trustees met in mid-September to decide who was

going to be assigned to which school. The teachers weren't told what school they would have until about two weeks before school opened. When Daddy came home after getting his assignment, as soon as he was past the gate, he started calling, "Mama, they have worked it, and I am out of a school." My sister Ruth and my mother were out in the yard, and even before my father got to them, it all was spilling out of him: Mable Carter had been assigned to Maddenville, and he had lost his teaching position in the neighborhood school. He was being sent to Richardsville—so far he'd have to drive the horse and wagon—and the school trustees had told him he had to maintain an average of twenty pupils a day to keep the school open. "I don't know how I'm going to do it," he was saying over and over.

Whenever Daddy was in trouble, he went to Culpeper to talk things over with his brother, Willis. Nathaniel Madden hadn't succeeded in making my father into a missionary, but my father's brother, Willis Jackson Madden, became the preacher in the family. Uncle Willis—"Preacher Madden" to several generations of the citizens of Culpeper—was the pastor of Antioch Baptist Church in the Negro section of town, and he also taught school there. He cultivated a full beard—in an era when it wasn't fashionable—to make himself look more "biblical." He did have the appearance of an Old Testament prophet and there are still men living—white as well as Negro—who as little mischief-making boys remember having some Old Testament wrath called down on their heads by the "Preacher."

It was to this Old Testament figure that Daddy took his problem, and Uncle Willis responded with the wisdom of Solomon. Uncle Willis heard the situation and asked him, "Well, Obed, how many children do you have?" and when Daddy counted up, there was Denny, Ruth, Sally, O.W., Melissa, Everett, Hannibal, T.O., and Nat. Only Nat and I—I was five, and Nat was only two—were still too young to go to school; our older brothers and sisters ranged from six-year-old Hannibal to Denny, aged seventeen. This gave Daddy seven students from his own children. There was a good part of his enrollment, but he said, "Willis, I don't have any way to transport them." All he had was a two-wheeled dogcart, with one seat. Two people could ride on the seat, and maybe Daddy could squeeze two more down by his feet, but that was all. But Uncle Willis settled it and told him, "Obed, I'll let you have my buggy."

So my father took his teaching assignment in Richardsville, driving his brother's buggy and with his own children forming a large percentage of the student body. Melissa had been staying with Grandma Stokes because she had trouble walking when she was very young, and Grandma Stokes could give her the extra attention that my mother couldn't with all her other children. She was now brought back from Manassas to join the rest of us, going to school in Richardsville to help make the roster.

My father was transferred from the Maddenville school to Richardsville in 1908, but within a few years many of the Negroes had moved away from the Richardsville area, so there finally weren't enough young children there to make the roster, even with my father supplying his own children as part of the roll.

By that time—around 1913—my sister Sally was also teaching in the area. She first taught at Stevensburg and then took over the school at Brandy Station. When her position at the Stevensburg school, which was closer to home than Richardsville, became available, my father took it. When Sally quit teaching, my father finished her term at the Brandy Station school. After a brief return to Richardsville, he finally returned to the Lignum school just after World War I, and he remained there until his retirement.

Culpeper County had only white school trustees—no school boards then and no separate boards for white and black schools. As far as I know, there weren't any colored school officials other than schoolteachers in Culpeper County.

Mr. Humphreys—Cary Humphreys—was one of the trustees. My sister Ruth remembers when his wife, Bena Humphreys, told Daddy, "The reason you are having so much trouble, Obed, is you are too smart for [to suit] them." Daddy could never really bring himself to believe this, but the rest of us knew that it was true. Negroes weren't supposed to be as intelligent as whites. They weren't supposed to be proud or ambitious. They were supposed to be happy to act as servants for whites. Our daddy was a smart, proud man, who didn't want to—and wouldn't—be a servant, and he didn't *teach* anybody to be a servant. And that's what the trustees didn't like.

Over time and with a bit of a nudge from my mother, my father bought his brother's interest in the farm and two more pieces of land, to square up the property. The first land he bought was in 1897, twenty acres, the site of the old Great Fork Church. Mary Doggett and her family had moved onto the property a few years before the Civil War began and lived in the old glebe house near the derelict church. The church had been gone since the time of the war, but the deed still called the land "the old Church tract." The Doggetts had taken squatters' rights. They paid the taxes on the land for more than forty years and claimed the land this way. The Doggett heirs sold the twenty acres to a woman named Nellie Woodlen for $125, but she had not paid all the money. My father finally bought the land by paying the balance and interest due on it—$19. It sounds like nothing, but that money was just as hard to come by as several thousand dollars now.

A year later he bought out his brother's interest in the old tavern tract. My daddy and his brother, Willis, each had a one-half interest in the farm after their mother's death. My parents were living on the farm; they had a spring box for cold springwater over the hill and were keeping the baby's milk in it. One Sunday Uncle Willis—this was before he was married, when he was something of a ladies' man—came with a girl friend and gave her the milk for her own child. Daddy had already gone to church. Then Mama found out that Uncle Willis had taken the milk—the milk from the cows that Mama took care of and that she had milked herself. My sister Ruth, who was six at the time, remembers that the children all were dressed for church, but they never got there. . . .

My parents were married over fifty years, and I never heard them quarrel, but Mama told Ruth the story after she was married, and Ruth told me. When Daddy came home from church, he was confronted by a furious Mama: "You either buy Willis out, or Willis buys you out, but I am not going to stand for him coming and giving our milk to that woman." The point was not negotiable; Mama had made up her mind.

It was in the summertime of 1898 that Mama took her stand about Daddy's buying Willis out or Willis's buying him out. Daddy was worried that he couldn't get enough money to buy the land, but Mama was ready for Daddy's worries. She had saved some money from her salary and from her egg business. She gave Daddy two hundred dollars, and they had bought Uncle Willis's share by the fall of the year.

In 1912 Daddy bought his last piece of land, another twenty acres, a part of the old Barbour land adjoining the tavern tract. The Barbour tract was originally five hundred acres of land. David Brown bought it for a dollar an acre and put a sawmill in and cut the lumber—railroad ties—out of the Barbour tract. Then he sold my father the cutover timberland from the Barbour tract that came up next to our homeplace. My father bought the twenty acres to keep people from moving into the back there and to square our place up. After he had cut all the timber out of the land, David Brown charged him ten dollars an acre, two hundred dollars for the twenty acres.

And where did my father get the money for the Barbour land? From his children: from the money that people had given us for presents and from the savings we earned as sextons, cleaning the Ebenezer Baptist Church.

All we children had little savings banks—the Second National Bank gave them out—little metal banks where we put our pennies and dimes and dollars. When people came in the summertime and gave us five cents or ten cents or fifty cents, my mother told us to put that money away in the little bank. We added whatever we made at jobs like cleaning the church, and at Christmas every year Mother carried that money to the bank and put it down to each account.

My mother figured out what we needed for the land, and we children—Denny, Sally, Ruth, Everett, and the rest of us—went ahead and got our money. Whatever we had been saving the money for, my father thought that the Barbour land was more important. We all were still minors, and my father legally controlled our money. My father took the money that his children had saved and bought the twenty acres of land.

Afterward David Brown said that he didn't know, when my father came up for the deed, that my father had the money. He told some of his friends that if he'd known my father had the money, he'd never have sold it to him because he didn't really want to sell it. He thought he'd sell the land and get it back—get part of the money and then get to take the land back, too. Or maybe even get a deed of trust on all that my father had, and get that, too.

That's something that my dad drilled into me: Never mortgage any land to buy more land. He always told me the story of a family of Clarks who owned land from Stevensburg to Brandy Station. They owned all the farms around—several thousand acres. They owned sawmills, and they had a hardware store in Culpeper. Then another farm came on the market, and they mortgaged all their land to buy this farm—and they lost every bit of it. It was in the depression during Cleveland's time, the panic of '93. My daddy always said you'd never get *him* to sign a note, and he'd never owe any debt.

Daddy always instilled it in us: Don't buy and charge, because he said that something would happen. It appeared that something always happened when you had something charged against you.

He remembered his grandfather Willis Madden. Willis Madden had so much money out on credit he couldn't have paid it. The war came on and wiped him out. He was compensated for some of his loss because he didn't raise arms against the United States government. Even so, Willis Madden didn't profit much by it. His son Samuel Madden was the one who negotiated for the money and handled it. Willis Madden was hoping to pay off his debtors, but before he could, he got old and feeble and finally lost his mind. Samuel Madden took part of that money and educated his own children. He didn't give it to my grandmother Maria because she had two illegitimate children, and he ostracized her because she didn't marry until after Daddy and Uncle Willis were born.

My father was difficult man. He was a proud man, an arrogant—very arrogant—man. He would say, "I'll talk right up to your teeth." He wasn't very diplomatic in his approach with the public, and he had a temper. He tended to go off half cocked—and not hit the target. He wanted to be an orator. He'd heard Frederick Douglass speak once, and my father wanted to be an orator with that power, but he didn't have the technique of his brother, Willis; he wasn't a good speaker. But he still could quote Scripture; he could quote passages from poems and classic books and plays. It was hard to argue with him; he was always ready with more quotes.

At Sunday school conventions he was always ready to

jump up and have his say, especially since he had developed great rivalries with some of the other churchmen. They'd get going at some of these conventions, and "I move" and "Brother Moderator" would be coming from all sides. And then my daddy would get up and say, "I call for a point of order"—to people who didn't know what a point of order meant.

My father was a great religious man. He went to church and the Sunday school conventions. He could recite the Beatitudes. But he never learned that "Blessed are the meek, for they shall inherit the earth."

Daddy had his own children listed on his classroom roster, but most of the time he kept his children at home working, to keep him in school teaching. I once had a long discussion with Ruth concerning our education and recorded what she said. Although she was talking about her own experience, it pretty much describes what we all had to do:

"Papa made it [our education] up to us. Denny and I had to sit down and study at night. All us children that could read read the Bible. And after we read the Bible, we had to write a story about what we had read. And Papa corrected that, as our English assignment, the next night. But I know I didn't sit down and do nothing, I learned all that I learned even if I didn't go to school, when I got large enough I stayed home and worked.

"The last year I was home—it was nineteen and oh-eight— I think I made twenty days in school. Because I had to see that the corn was cut, and you had eight rows to a shock— really sixteen rows: eight rows on a side, and you had to cut that corn and throw it down and shock it up. And then I had to harrow that land and put that wheat in, ten, twelve acres of wheat.

"In nineteen and oh-eight I sowed all the wheat, I saw that the corn was gotten in, I saw that the wood was in—I think we sawed the wood up stove length in the woods. I hauled it in in a one-horse wagon. Papa hired me out to

Peter Ross [a neighbor], and I sowed wheat for him. He would tell me how many pecks—in other words, he would say, 'put five pecks to the acre.' You knew how much, and you had a little cart, and you put this wheat in there, in the front, and in the back was fertilizer, so many pounds to the acre for the fertilizer. And I sowed all the wheat at home wherever Papa said sow it, sowed all the rye wherever he said sow it. Then I went down to Peter Ross's and sowed wheat or whatever he wanted down there. And then I had to get the wood in, and I only put twenty days in school then, and school closed the last day in February."

My father never could or did realize that he sacrificed his children so that he could teach school. We had to stay home and shuck the corn and get the wood in, while he was going off and teaching other people's children. My sister Ruth has always believed that my parents' teaching us at home, in the evenings, made our education up to us. But some of us, especially my brother O.W. and myself, always felt a little cheated. It was mighty hard to face a long day of work in the fields while we watched Daddy going down the road, on his way to give other children the education that we weren't getting.

My father had begun teaching at the Lignum school and finished his teaching career there as well. The school closed when he retired in 1936. When my father finally quit teaching, he got more money as retirement than he did teaching because he got money every month. He got paid for only six or seven months when he was teaching school. The highest he ever got paid for teaching school was forty-five dollars a month for the term. But he got seventy-five dollars a month pension, each month, twelve months a year. He was seventy-six years old when he retired; he had been teaching for fifty-five consecutive years.

My mother died in 1944, and my father in 1949. They were married for fifty-four years. My sister Denny and I lived at home and took care of the house and the farm. To

T. O. Madden, Sr., and his wife, Landonia, on the occasion of their fiftieth wedding anniversary in 1940.

the end of his life my father never would do "servant's work." He made somebody work for him, or it didn't get done. He lived to be eighty-nine years old, and I never saw him cook a meal, wash a dish, wash clothes, or sweep a floor at home. My mother, Denny, my wife, or I did the work, or if all else failed, he had women from the neighborhood do the housework or wash clothes at times, but to the end of his life he never did "servant's work"—even for himself.

My father was a self-taught, self-made man. Most of the education he had he taught himself or he worked to pay for it. I've heard the expression that anybody self-taught or self-made is always praising his maker. That was my father. The only formal education he had was when he was a young teenager at his uncle Nat's and when he came back and went to the Summer Institutes. But my father always had a chronic idea of teaching—telling you what *he* knew. He never was concerned with *you*. But he would always tell you what he thought. My sister Ruth has a lot of our father in her. If you tell her something, she has to come back with something to top it: "That doesn't beat *mine*—I've got one. . . ." That was my father, too.

When I was kidding Ruth about that, she started to come back with another "topper": "Now, T.O., I'm like Papa enough—I prided myself in teaching a person etiquette. . . ."

And I just had to tell her that was my father's greatest asset: My father could teach music, but he never could play a piano.

Postscript to Chapter Eight

A FEW NOTES ON MY BROTHERS AND SISTERS

֍

Each of Thomas Obed Madden, Sr.'s children was taught by him; they received what formal elementary education they got from their father. The oldest ones—Odenla (Denny), Ruth, Sally, Oliver Wendell (O.W.), and Everett—first attended the school near Maddenville and then, after my father was moved to Richardsville, went with him to that school.

My oldest sister, Denny, was a student of my father, first at the school near Maddenville and then at Richardsville. She attended until she was about seventeen or eighteen. The family did not think that she was college material, so her formal training stopped at that point.

After leaving the Richardsville school, Ruth, the next sister, went to Virginia Normal, which is now Virginia State College, in Petersburg for four years. After she had graduated from Virginia Normal, her first job was teaching at a school in Glen Allen in Henrico County in 1913. She later taught in Hanover and Fauquier counties.

My sister Sally, after leaving school in Richardsville, went down to the Manassas Industrial School for four years, returned to the county of Culpeper, was employed as a teacher at Stevensburg and then at Brandy Station. After leaving Brandy Station, she went down to work as a supervisor in a laundry that was run by her cousin Oceola ("Ocie") Madden. From there she moved to Washington, D.C., and became employed in the Bureau of Printing and Engraving of the United States government.

When my brother O.W. left the school at Richardsville, he became an apprentice to a blacksmith, Dick Burton, in Stevensburg. After that he went down to the Hampton Institute for two years. At that time, during the First World War, the army was looking for Negroes to be trained as officers. O.W. was selected as one of the candidates for Officers Training School, which he attended out in Chillicothe, Ohio. (There were three white fellows from our area, Ab Willis's grandsons, who also were in the war. They were discharged as either corporals or sergeants, and O.W. was discharged as a second lieutenant.) O.W. later owned and operated a grocery store in Washington, D.C., until his retirement..

My brother Everett left the Richardsville school at the time Sally was teaching in the county, so he went to school in Stevensburg, riding shotgun with her. Then, after that, he went down to Tuskegee Institute in Alabama for a year. From Tuskegee he went out to Indiana, where he worked in the Studebaker plant, and he never returned to Culpeper.

My sister Melissa stayed with her grandmother down in Manassas for a couple of years and then returned to school in Richardsville. At the age of about eighteen, which was during the First World War, she had a job teaching at The Forest, a Negro community near Crooked Run Church in Culpeper County.

The next brother, Hannibal, also went to school with our

The author's five sisters. From left to right: Sarah, Melissa, Landonia, Odenla, and Ruth.

father, at Richardsville and later at Stevensburg. Then, like our brother O.W., he became an apprentice to the black-smith Dick Burton. After this he went down to the District of Columbia and worked in the grocery store that our brother O.W. owned and operated. Hannibal worked in the grocery store with O.W., and later he worked for several contractors as a carpenter and a plasterer. Hannibal worked as a blacksmith for the government in Washington, D.C., during World War II. He later became a self-employed contractor for carpentry and plastering.

Next was T.O.—myself, Thomas Obed, Jr. The next chapter is my story, so I'm not giving myself another paragraph here.

My younger brother, Nat, went to school at my father's last posts, Stevensburg and Lignum. After leaving Lignum, he went to D.C., where he received employment as a mortician. That didn't turn out too well, and he finally became self-employed as an exterminator.

My youngest sister, Landonia, also went to school in Lignum, but she went to high school in D.C. and later married and remained there.

Chapter Nine

T. O. MADDEN, JR.'S STORY

🙝🙟

. . . *So you want to know when T.O. was born? I'll tell you like I told the people who wanted me to fill out the question so T.O. could get his passport. I put when he was born, the date and the year and where, and his mother's name and his father's name and gave it to T.O. They wrote on there they wanted to know if I really knew when T.O. was born and if I could tell them anything about T.O.'s birth. So I sat down and wrote:*

I wrote that Sarah Stokes, the mother of Landonia Stokes Madden, came up to granny the baby, and my mother wasn't having the baby soon enough. And my grandmother raised turkeys, and she believed in looking after her turkeys. I heard them talking, "Donie, I've got to go back," Grandma said, "I've got to go back home today, 'cause I've got to look after my turkeys." She didn't say turkeys—it was "tai-keys." My mother got out in the garden with a hoe, got out there in the morning of the tenth of July, nineteen hundred and three. And she worked her sweet potatoes all day long. And T.O. was born sometime after twelve o'clock [midnight] of the eleventh—the next morning—after Mama had chopped the garden all day long on the tenth. T.O. was born sometime between twelve o'clock and early in the morning on the eleventh, 'cause Papa called us in the morning: "Denny, Ruth—come on down, you've got a little brother."

*And then he had to go and hook up his horse to the cart and take
Grandma Stokes right to the train that went through Brandy at twelve
something. Grandma Stokes left T.O. as a baby before he was one
day old, because she had done her job of delivering him, and she had
to get back to those "tai-keys."*

*And we—Denny and I—had to take care of T.O., because Mama
had what you called a milk leg and she couldn't walk. And T.O. was
very, very fretful, so we—Denny and I—went to the store at Lignum
and bought a bottle of Mellin's Food [a well-known commercial baby
food of the time] and a nursery bottle that had a little glass contrap-
tion that went down in the bottom and went up and stuck in the
cork, and the cork then had a nipple on it, and we followed the directions and made the Mellin's Food, and gave it to T.O. that afternoon
after we bought it, and T.O. was the best baby. He'd just go asleep,
and he slept. He was one good baby, one of the best babies that
Mama had, so far as not crying and sleeping. Denny or I would hold
the baby over a basin while the other washed him. I was eleven and
Denny was twelve. We already had experience—see, we had the charge
of the baby when Hannibal was born [in January 1902]. And Denny
and I took care of T.O.*

*Ruth Madden Alexander, July 11, 1988
(speech made at T. O. Madden, Jr.'s eighty-fifth
birthday party)*

A nd as for the last chapter, well, that's my life—and I
lived it. . . .

I was born poor, dirt poor, in Culpeper County in 1903.
It was hard times. It was right after the start of Jim Crow,
complete segregation by law, something that even Willis
Madden never had to contend with. We were caught in the
middle. Whites wouldn't accept us because we had Negro
blood. Negroes said we acted like we thought we were better than they were because we lived differently: We owned
our farm and tried to get educated.

I'm looking back on eighty-seven years of life. I've seen a

lot of changes in my time. I've lived long enough to see the modern world, to see automobiles and planes and space travel, and to see integration come and some of the old barriers breaking down.

I started school in Richardsville in 1909, when I was six years old, with my father as my teacher. Daddy had to keep up his roll. He had to recruit all his children that were school age (or anywhere near it), so he took me along. He needed another student, since that was the year that my sister Denny stopped going to school, and Ruth left the county to go away to teachers' college. And so I came of school age.

I went to school decked out in my new red coat, sent down in one of the barrels from our Stokes relatives. It was a girl's coat, but I was thankful for it anyhow; it kept me warm in all but the coldest weather. I went to school until Christmas, because after Christmas it was so cold sitting in the buggy you'd freeze to death going to school. Even my red coat didn't help then.

I went to Richardsville to my father's school for a while, and later, when he was teaching at the Stevensburg school, I went there for a little while longer, but I spent a lot of time at home when I was needed to help on the farm. My mother or father would teach me in the evenings or when there were no chores to be done. Whenever any of us were working at home, my mother would have us come in when there was nothing to do and give us lessons. I got most of my schooling between farm work—between shucking the corn, sowing the wheat, and getting in the wood for the winter months. For ages fourteen and fifteen I did go to school in the winter months—January, February, and a part of March. After I became sixteen, my formal education stopped. I just never went back to school. I quit school when I was able to plow; I was too old for schooling because I was old enough for heavy farm work.

About the time that I quit school, there was the big influenza epidemic of 1918. It was a terrible time—like a biblical plague over the face of the land. Nearly every household had the illness. Everybody at home had the flu except Mama. Nobody was sure what caused the sickness. People were trying everything from science to superstition to keep from getting it. Some people tried wearing masks; some hung bags of medicine around their necks. Some put sulfur in their shoes.

Ruth came home from her teaching job in Henrico County to help at home. Since the rest of us were sick, Ruth had to milk the cows. There was no dairy then; you carried a little stool and milked the cows where you found them. The cows were used to being milked by the boys; they wouldn't let Ruth near them until she put on a pair of pants.

Ruth and Mama tried sprinkling sulfur inside their shoes to keep the flu away, and Mama didn't let Ruth go near the family members sick with the flu. Maybe it did some good. Mama and Ruth didn't get sick, and the rest of us recovered. We were the only family in the neighborhood who didn't lose a member. Some people lost half their families.

There used to be two colored schools in the neighborhood—the ones my parents taught at. Then the community thinned out. The older colored people died; the young people went away to school or work and never came back. When I came along, the sawmills and farming were the only employ. Most of those people who had children were tenants living on all those farms. Then, after the First World War, the young people went away to the factories in Philadelphia and Baltimore. There was a place near Baltimore called Sparrows Point where they worked in the steel mills. Then some of the people who were educated worked in the government; you could make a good salary in the government.

I worked on the farm until I was twenty-two; then I thought I'd try the city, too. I left to go to work for my

brother O.W. in Washington, D.C. I worked for O.W. from
October 1925 until August 1926, the first time I was ever
away from home. There I was—a country boy, a dumb
country boy—in the big city.

I went down on the train, from Brandy to Washington,
and O.W. met me there at Union Station. He lived up there
in Northeast—Forty-eighth Street and D Avenue Northeast. O.W. was running a grocery at Forty-eighth Street,
and I started there as a clerk in his store. He had also
befriended an old man who had a store on Fiftieth Street,
and when the man died, he bought the property from the
estate and set me up in that store. I put my own money into
the business. Then O.W. had to move, so he came into the
store where I was and put me out. He had started me running that store in April, and in August I was a retired boy.
He locked me out, and I had to come on back home.

I wrote my mother that O.W. had locked me out of the
store. She wrote back and told me that I could get something to eat, and I could find a place to sleep, if I wanted to
come back to it, but that's all she had to offer me. And like
she told my sister Ruth, when she looked, I was there.

People told me that I invested all the money I had and
got robbed, and I ought to hold O.W. responsible. But I
said no, I'd learned a lot. So I just marked it up as profit
and loss. I *had* learned a lot: You couldn't trust anybody.

In the country the way I was raised, your word was your
bond. Nobody put anything into written contracts; you just
gave your word.

Not so in Washington. I saw business done by some sharp
businessmen, like O.W. and some of the Jewish store-
keepers up there. If you went into a Jewish store—say, one
of the mom-and-pop stores—and you wanted a pound of
cheese, they had a finger on the scale if you didn't watch
them. And if you got home and found out and went back
to complain, they'd tell you, "But you saw me weigh it."

But they got careful if they knew you were going to check on them. They were good businessmen, true businessmen, but you couldn't trust them.

After I came home from the city, I began to get into the dairy and produce business. It just happened gradually. I sold eggs and butter from the farm. I first started shipping eggs to Washington, to a wholesaler there. But having been down on the street, at the wholesale market, I had caught on. I had learned how to sell a little bit. I was always venturing.

I came back from Washington in 1926, and I started farming. My father was still teaching, and he said, "I can teach, but you, you're going to break down." He figured that I wasn't fitted for a career, not for anything except farm work. But I told my father, "You can teach, but you do not have enough contact with the folks; it's more than reading and writing."

My mother still was keeping hens. The average person, up to the depression, kept fifty or sixty hens, and would have up to five to ten dozen eggs a week to sell.

My mother and I started to sell eggs to Washington, D.C. We'd ship eggs to O.W., since he was in the store business, but he was slow in paying. And then we began to separate cream. We started to make and sell butter and then started selling cream, too. Every farmer—every professional farmer—was buying a few cows. We started with five or six cows, then worked up to about ten or fifteen.

Instead of shipping our produce, I began to take it to Washington myself. I ran my route once a week: left home Thursday night, arrived in D.C. on Friday morning, and sold my eggs door to door. My brother Nat knew some people. They helped get me started. Then I just expanded on word of mouth.

I started this business right during the depression, the last year of Hoover's administration. I was in Washington that day in 1932 when General MacArthur drove the Bonus

Army out. They were camped all around Washington, waiting for their bonus. They got a bond, but it wasn't due, and those men—who had been soldiers—wanted their money now.

The old veterans came there and camped in Washington, and then Hoover had the army drive them out. We were sitting at a corner with the produce truck when the soldiers came by, breaking up the bonus marchers. Some of these men were nearly broke, with no money to buy food or get home; they were trying to raise money by selling whatever they had. One of the bonus marchers sold me a good watch for sixty-five cents.

By the time of the depression I had a thriving business selling country produce on the streets in Washington, D.C.: eggs, butter, buttermilk, produce, and some meat. I churned my cream in a Maytag washer and sold the "country butter"—sweet butter, with no salt—in Washington. The Jewish people bought it; they didn't want any salt, and they cooked with butter.

Most of my business, my customers, were Jews. They had their places of business down on Seventh Street—secondhand clothing stores and so on. That's where I sold a lot of my produce, on Seventh Street. You couldn't sell them a dressed chicken; they bought the chicken live and then took it to the rabbi to be killed and dressed, kosher. They wanted fresh eggs, chickens, and the sweet country butter.

I did both retail and wholesale. I'd get extra eggs from Mrs. Annie Reynolds in Richardsville—wholesale, nine cents a dozen. She had a colored girl helping to wash and iron, Betty Hays, and she got twenty-five cents a day.

I raised my own eggs and other produce and bought more wholesale when I needed to. If I bought wholesale, I'd pay nine to twelve cents a dozen. I sold them to the wholesalers for fifteen cents. I sold them retail to the housewives in D.C. for anywhere from twenty-five up to forty-five cents a dozen; I retailed for whatever the section of town would pay. You'd be in the colored section, and you could get one price for your produce; then you'd go up on, say, Connecticut Avenue, and prices could go up. You got whatever you could get for it.

I had what we called a jumper—a boy to come with me and help me—and he said, "Mr. T.O., you ain't honest. You sell eggs to some of them for twenty-five cents and forty-five cents to others." And I told him, "Well, maybe these eggs are worth twenty-five cents to you here, but they're worth forty-five cents to him over there. It's whatever you can get. I can't carry 'em back. I've got to sell them because the hens are laying at home."

When I was going back and forth with my produce, I had a Ford half-ton pickup truck. It had a canvas top on it, and I put a rack on it. I'd go out there and load it down with eggs, chickens, potatoes. I took both live chickens (for the Jewish market) and dressed chickens. I'd dress about a hundred or so chickens. At that time you didn't draw a chicken (take the intestines out) for market. You just picked them. The head, the feet, everything else was on, everything but the feathers.

I had my produce route when there were still general stores. You could pay in money or produce at the local stores; if you wanted coffee or sugar, you'd take a chicken in and trade it. Then the big stores started coming. The first of those stores was Piggly Wiggly, and then there was A&P and the Safeway store. You had to wait on yourself in those. When I was raised, in the time of the old general stores and in the grocery store where I worked, a person didn't touch that produce. It was all behind the counter, you told the clerk what you wanted, and he got it for you. But when you came in the Piggly Wiggly store, you had to get the groceries yourself. The clerk was at the door, and he checked you out—to save labor, they said. In a country store the clerk had to wait on the people, but now, in the big stores, you have to wait on yourself.

I stopped my butter and produce runs about 1936. The farm was getting bigger, and there was getting to be too much to do at home. I could make more profits at home looking after things there. My parents were getting older, too.

About 1936 I started milking and selling milk in Culpeper. This was the last year my father was teaching, and I hired the Myrtle children, some of his students, to help me. They milked the cows and carried the cream and milk with me every morning. After the cows were milked, we had about five cans of milk, which held forty or fifty gallons of milk. I made a rack on the back of my truck to hold the cans, and we milked the cows and carried the milk to the creamery each day before the children went to school.

The farming that I was doing in the 1930s was different from the farming that I had done as a boy and different from the practice of farming today. I saw farming become mechanized within my lifetime. I can remember people who used oxen for draft animals. By the time that I was born, farmers didn't plow land with oxen much—too slow. But they used them in the woods, for logging, and years ago there was a man called David Jacobs, who did custom threshing, and he used steam engines. He had six oxen to pull that big steam engine around, and they'd hook it up with belts to the threshing machine. That was round about 1910. I was a little bitty boy about seven years old. I used to go out and help the man early in the morning to round those oxen up. They had a rope on their horns to lead them, and you took a prick—a sharp stick—and you hit the oxen on the horns if you wanted them to go one way, and you hit them on the other side to turn them the other way. And after we brought them in, they were hitched up to the traction engine, to pull it to where it had to go.

I never did plow with oxen, only horses. But every saw-mill used oxen in the woods, for pulling logs. And they were used to pull things like the steam engines. The old-timers talked about using oxen for other purposes as well— to plow, to pull carts, and haul loads in heavy, wet ground. It had been like that for hundreds of years, but it was ending by the time that I came along.

My parents used horses on the farm, to harrow and plow, do the other field work, and pull our farm wagon and buggy.

I first went from horses to tractors in 1926 or '27. There was a family up in Culpeper, by the name of Daingerfield, and they had a Titan 1020 tractor. Old man Daingerfield died, and they had to settle his estate. Jim Swan, the tractor dealer, still had a $100 note on this Titan tractor, and he had a sheriff's sale. They sold the tractor at public auction, and I bought the tractor for $110. Daingerfield had paid $1,200 for it.

It was too big and awkward to plow with, but I used it for disking the fields, and I ran a threshing machine with it. Then after that I went to a F-14 International tractor. I traded for a F-14, and that pulled a one-bottom plow.

I never had one of the big steam engines. I didn't know anything about steam engines. When I got into power, it was gasoline. Steam was too big and awkward for these small farms. The International people first came out with the F-12, but that wasn't quite big enough, so then they came out with a little larger tractor, the F-14. Then came the bigger tractors that could handle two plows, and then three plows. But I started out with the old 1020 and then the F-14. I traded ten cows for my F-14.

By the time that I retired from farming at age eighty, we were using tractors bigger and more sophisticated and more powerful than anything that I could have imagined when I was young. The modern tractors are almost as far removed from the early models as the old 1020 and F-14 were from oxen and horses.

I had some money saved when the depression came along, and I was able to make some more with my produce route to Washington. I put my money into the most solid investment that I knew of: land. Few people were thinking my way. It was a time when a lot of people were selling their land or were going broke from mortgages, and their land was being auctioned off. They were selling, I was buying.

The first piece of land that I bought was the old Treat Ford place. David Campbell had bought it and put a deed of trust on the land. He married a widow, Roberta ("Bert") Bundy, and they were living in her house up in Bundytown. In May 1928 a tornado came through Bundytown. It blew the old Bundy place to pieces, and with it the Campbells. They found Bert Bundy under the steps, dead, and David Campbell out in the yard, with a piece of the cooking stove right through his forehead. When the family settled the estate, they sold the Treat Ford place to pay off the deed of trust, and I bought it: twenty-four acres for a little less than four hundred dollars. The year was 1930.

That was the start. After that I bought other small farms next to my property. There was the old Peter Ross place, thirty acres. Next was the Doggett place, just under sixteen acres. People told me that I was getting greedy about buying land, but like I told them, I wasn't greedy, I just wanted the land that adjoined mine.

I bought the John Brown place in 1935: 101 acres, sold at auction at the courthouse to settle his estate. The Browns had borrowed twelve hundred dollars from the Federal Land Bank to build the house, and the farm sold for the twelve hundred dollars. There were other parcels like this, too.

I bought my mother's old homeplace, the old Stokes place near Manassas, and after my wife's parents had died, I bought their house in Purcellville, in northern Virginia.

In 1949 my father died and left the homeplace, 135 acres, to myself and my sister Odenla.

During the recession in the 1960s, I bought more land

and added over four hundred more acres to my property.

The old people, farmers, had these places. When they got too old to operate the farms, and the young people moved to Washington and got jobs there, the land was sold. I had a total of about a thousand acres at greatest extent, with the land in three counties: Culpeper, Loudon, and Prince William.

Like my dad drilled into me, I never mortgaged any of my land to buy any more land. I always paid for it, always put my foot on what I had, and reached over and stepped on the other, but always kept my one foot on what I had. My lawyer was looking at some of my back records and told me that I was different from any of the other clients: With all the land I own, I never had a deed of trust on any of it.

I married Hazel Brown, a teacher from Purcellville in Loudon County, on October 31, 1942. I was forty years old. We had four children: Thomasene, born September 9, 1943; T.O. III ("Obed"), born August 17, 1946; a daughter, stillborn in 1947; and William ("Billy"), born January 11, 1949.

I was dairy farming, and then I expanded into beef cattle. I raised grain and hay, too, but only for feed; everything went back into the cows. I made good money at it, but we never lived in much style. I was still investing my money—in two ways now: I was buying land with my money and investing money in my children, too. I gave my children the best education that I could.

Most of my family, since the days of Sarah Madden, have been Baptists. Most of us took our faith seriously. Sarah Madden and her family rode, or even walked, all the way to the Mount Pony church near Culpeper. Willis Madden gave the land for the first Ebenezer Church in the neighborhood, and his son Samuel was a preacher. My father and mother were very religious. My uncle Willis was a preacher. I was baptized in the Baptist Church. But when

Thomas Obed Madden, Jr., and his wife, Hazel.

I married and started raising a family, I didn't feel that I was capable of giving my kids the religious education that they needed. The Ebenezer Church minister at the time had a fifth-grade education; the Sunday school teachers could barely read and write. Their horizons were limited. They didn't have the vision to prepare my children for what I felt they would need in their future. Like Sarah and Willis Madden before me, I wanted my children to rise in the world.

My mother died when my first child was just a baby, and my two oldest children were just getting to the age when they could start Sunday school when my father died. I knew that if I sent my children elsewhere, I couldn't hurt my parents now. I asked my sister Landonia what I should do, and she said, "Take your children to the Catholic Church." I knew that one of the clerks in the local hardware store was a Catholic. I talked with him, and he helped arrange for the priest to come out to talk with us. In those days there were only about twenty people at mass at Precious Blood Church in Culpeper every week.

Just as the religious education at Precious Blood Church was superior to that at Ebenezer Church, the Catholic Church's private schools offered a much better education to my children than the local segregated schools. I sent my daughter Thomasene to St. Dominic's Grade School in New Jersey, and she was baptized in the Catholic Church. My son Obed was also baptized soon after. Soon people at the Precious Blood Church in Culpeper told me that my wife and I should follow their lead, and we did.

I continued my children's education in private Catholic schools, mostly in the North and in Canada. I was in a position to prepare them to compete in the world, and I wanted them to have freedom of choice in their life—to be able to become whatever they wanted. They wouldn't have had too much choice in the segregated schools in Culpeper. I had another reason for sending my children away to school, too: I wanted to see that they got a wider view of the world. I remembered my first experience in Washington—coming in as a green country boy and getting cheated. I knew that my children needed a good education but that reading and writing weren't enough: You had to have contact with different kinds of people and learn to cope with them.

You might say that our conversion to Catholicism was from an educational standpoint. As a result of their education in Catholic church schools, my children have gained more recognition than anything I could have thought of or hoped for them.

One of the most significant events that I saw in my life was the end of segregation. The younger people today are not aware of what segregation was like. Unless you have experienced segregation, there are things that can't be explained, that can't be expressed in words—things that you have to have felt. Unless you have actually lived through segregation, unless you have experienced it firsthand, you can never know exactly what it was like. But I can make a few observations on what segregation was.

Segregation was someone's assuming that you are different and not quite as good as he was; only it wasn't just someone's opinion, it was the law.

Segregation was when I used to be driving to Culpeper, and I'd stop to pick up a little white boy walking along and give him a lift to town. He could ride on the seat beside me. I could give him a nickel to buy himself a Coke in one of the stores. I could go into the store and get one for myself. The little boy could stay in the store, sit down, and have his drink there. I'd have to leave the store and go outside to have my drink.

Segregation was an incident when I was first married, when my wife, Hazel, went to the town of Culpeper. She went into Gayheart's Drug Store and ordered lunch. She was served at the lunch counter, her food came on a china plate, and her drink in a glass, and she sat down and ate it there. The other colored people complained: "Mrs. Madden gets served here, but I can't." The people working the lunch counter had seen a good-looking, well-dressed, light-skinned lady come in and order a meal, and they had served her at the counter. They hadn't known that she was colored, hadn't known what her name was. The next time she went back, they served her, not on a plate but in a paper cup, and she had to take it out of the store to eat.

I don't know whether I was fortunate or unfortunate to know in what poor esteem the average Negro was held. Because of the light color of my skin, I heard things that a lot of Negroes didn't hear, from white speakers who didn't know that there were any Negroes in the audience.

Segregation was regardless of your age, regardless of your station in life, regardless of how hard you worked. It considered only one thing. Having lived through segregation, I know exactly how Jesus felt when Peter denied Him.

When the laws changed and the civil rights movement came, I'm not sure that integration itself meant that much to me. The important thing to me wasn't that integration had finally come; it was that segregation had ended.

Hazel and I did the opposite of what my parents had done: I ran the farm, and Hazel taught school. She taught at the Maddenville school until she retired. The Maddenville school had begun with a Madden—my mother—and it ended with our family, too. When Hazel retired, on June 14, 1965, the Maddenville school closed forever. It was the last one-room school in Culpeper County.

Hazel was blind the last seven years of her life before she died in 1983. I began to wonder whether my time was running out, too. There were things that I still wanted to do. I began to put together all my notes on my family history. I took my first fling at publication and put out a booklet on Willis Madden and his tavern—the forerunner of this book.

I made a successful application to get the old tavern recognized as a landmark to Willis Madden and his achievements. Madden's tavern was placed on the Virginia Landmarks Register and on the National Register of Historic Places in 1984.

On my eightieth birthday—July 11, 1983—I had to walk three miles home in hundred-degree heat after my old car quit on me. And I thought that for once in my life I'd like to go in style. I didn't want to be like Moses and have to die before I could enter the promised land. I replaced my old car, with 150,000 miles on it, and my old pickup truck, which wasn't any better, with some new vehicles that weren't always breaking down. I remodeled the house a little.

I retired from farming at age eighty. I've got some of the farm rented out, and I've turned the rest over to my children. I sold my property in northern Virginia, and with that money I decided that I'd finally have a little of the good life—in my eighties.

I've done some traveling—taken some cruises and gone to see some far parts of the world. So far I've been to Ireland, England, eastern Canada, British Columbia, Hawaii, Nassau, Mexico, Arizona, California, Chicago, New York City, and up and down the East Coast of the United States. I've already visited Australia, New Zealand, and Paris, France, during the last half of my eighties. And there are still a lot more places that I want to see.

You might have seen my picture in the September 1987 *National Geographic*, in the article on President James Madison. The Maddens are the only Negro family currently documented to descend from a servant proved to have belonged to the Madison family. No descendants of Madison slaves have been documented.

In the fall of 1987 I decided to retrace the steps that Mary Madden had taken so long ago. I took a tour of Ireland. There are plenty of Maddens there still. I rented a Mercedes car—a little different from the way that Mary Madden would have traveled—and went through nineteen counties. Then I took a plane and flew over to England. In a restaurant in London I noticed a man staring at me. Finally he came over and apologized for interrupting my meal, but he just had to know: "Excuse me sir, but didn't I see your picture in *National Geographic*?"

I'd come a long way from a poor country boy in Culpeper County, Virginia.

Finally, I decided to tell my family's story—and add my own story—and get it into print. That is how this book came to be.

There are always people who are jealous. My father had to deal with them, and so did Willis Madden, and probably so did Sarah Madden. I've had people tell me, "T.O., I'm going to see you on your way down when I'm on my way up." But people have been saying that to me for seventy years. They've been saying, "T.O.'s all for himself." Well, I guess I am, but who am I going to be for? I've seen many

The author plays with some of his dogs in the yard of the historic Madden family home. Photo, Stephen W. Sylvia.

things in my life. I've done the best I could by my children. I've written a book. I've been able to meet intelligent people and enjoy myself some, and whether good or bad, I've seen a little of the world. When you come right down to it, the Lord's been good to me.

NOTES

꒰꒱

The following abbreviations are used throughout the notes:

CCC: Culpeper County Circuit Court Clerk's office. Culpeper, Virginia.

MCC: Madison County Circuit Court Clerk's office, Madison, Virginia.

OCC: Orange County Circuit Court Clerk's office, Orange, Virginia.

SCC: Spotsylvania County Circuit Court Clerk's office, Spotsylvania, Virginia.

UVA University of Virginia, Charlottesville, Virginia.

VSLA: Virginia State Library Archives, Richmond, Virginia.

All family documents and information on family legends cited in the text are in the collection of the author unless otherwise noted. Original spelling and usage have been retained in these documents.

page
1   Laws concerning mulatto children: See W. W. Hening, ed. *The Statutes at Large: Being a Collection of All the Laws of Virginia* (Richmond, 1823), v. II, p. 260, and v. III, p. 87.
3   Vestry accounts concerning Mary Madden: St. George's

Parish Vestry Book, pp. 108, 125, 126; Special Collections, Alderman Library, UVA.

11 George Fraser's inventory: Spotsylvania County Will Book D, p. 259, SCC.

12 *Madison v. Fraser's Executrix:* Orange County Order Book 7, p. 463, and Orange County judgments, November Court, 1767, OCC.

12 The copy of Sarah's indenture papers, addressed to "Col. Madison," was signed by William Underwood, who was clerk of the vestry of St. George's Parish only between 1768 and 1770; the copy of Sarah's indenture papers therefore had to be made in those years: St. George's Parish Vestry Book, UVA.

17 James Madison, Sr.'s, Personal Property tax records: Orange County Personal Property tax lists, VSLA.

17 The 1765 law governing terms of servitude: Hening, *Statutes,* v. 8, p. 133.

19 The 1788 law fixing the death penalty for selling a free Negro as a slave: Ibid., v. 12, p. 531.

20 James Mercer's letter to Colonel James Madison, Sr.: Shane Collection, Presbyterian Historical Society, Philadelphia, Pennsylvania.

23 For the younger James Madison's letter, see William T. Hutchinson et al., eds., *The Papers of James Madison* (Chicago, Charlottesville, 1962–), v. 8, p. 304.

23 The will of James Madison, Sr.: Orange County Will Book 4, p. 1, OCC.

24 The deed from James Madison, Sr., to Francis Madison: Culpeper County Deed Book M, p. 206, CCC. Francis Madison's Personal Property tax records: See Culpeper County Personal Property tax lists, VSLA.

25 Francis Madison's inventory: Madison County Will Book 1, p. 283, MCC.

36 Free Negro marriages as common-law relationships: See John B. Minor, *Institutes of Common and Statute Law,* 4th ed., (Richmond, 1892), v. I, p. 68.

43 The will of John Hackley: Culpeper County Will Book D, p. 321, CCC.

43 Oliver Bannister: Orange County Minute Book 2, p. 171;

March 28, 1782, OCC. An Oliver Banister also appears as
the administrator of the estate of an Arther Banister, perhaps his father, in 1794: Orange County Minute Book 3,
p. 205, Orange County, OCC. If this is the same Oliver
Bannister (also spelled Banister in some documents) who
later lived in Culpeper County, it suggests that he was the
child of free Negroes and had been bound out as the result
of his parents' poverty.

43 The will of John Barnes: Culpeper County Will Book D,
p. 267, CCC.

64 Deeds concerning the old Barnes land are recorded at Culpeper County Deed Books XX, p. 200; Deed Book YY,
p. 38; Deed Book 2, p. 41 and (for Willis Madden's purchase) Deed Book 2, p. 402), CCC.

73 Culpeper Legislative Petitions: VSLA.

73 ". . . the very drones and pests of society": See Thomas
R. Dew, *Review of the Debate in the Virginia Legislature of
1831 and 1832* (Richmond, 1832).

74 Restrictions on Negroes' keeping taverns: *1830 Code of
Virginia*, p. 247, and the *1860 Code of Virginia*, p. 224.

94 French Madden's presence on the railroad crew: Culpeper
County Personal Property taxes, 1851, VSLA.

103 Heros von Borcke's account of Pelham's visit to Madden's
tavern is given in his *Memoirs of the Confederate War for
Independence*, 2 vols. (London, 1866).

119 Census entry concerning H. Rollin Lucas: 1880 Culpeper
County Census (Stevensburg District, p. 21). For a short
overview of Freedmen's Bureau records of these and other
schools in Culpeper County, see Eugene M. Scheel, *Culpeper: A Virginia County's History through 1920* (Culpeper,
Culpeper County Historical Society, 1982) pp. 218, 418.

120 Willis Madden's deed to Jack Madden: Culpeper County
Deed Book 17, p. 554, CCC.

122 Disposition of Willis Madden's estate: Under Willis Madden's will, the house and surrounding land had been left
jointly to Maria and to his granddaughter Margaret (or
Marguerite) Taylor, but Margaret died young, before Willis, and her share of the property went into his estate. Maria
purchased the remaining acreage, minus the 0.5 acre that

had been given to the church and the 6.2 acres that had previously been sold to Edward Burrell (Culpeper County Deed Book 20, p. 328, CCC) in early 1883. The deed to Maria is recorded in the Culpeper County Deed Book 20, p. 452, CCC. The total of all the parcels of land from Willis Madden's property, including Jack Madden's 10.75 acres, was actually a little over 112 acres, 25 acres more than was shown on the survey of the Barnes estate when Willis Madden first bought the land.

139– Deeds to T. O. Madden, Sr.: Culpeper County Deed Book
140 29, p. 150; 30, p. 37; and 49, p. 173, CCC.

Appendix One

SELECTED
DOCUMENTS

~~~

BIRTH RECORDS

Birth records from the Madden papers list Sarah Madden's children and grandchildren. It seems that after Sarah had lived in Culpeper County for several years, one of her employers, merchant William Banks, contacted Francis Madison to get documentation of the children's ages (probably at Sarah's urging). He witnessed the copy that Francis Madison made, probably from farm records. Later Banks, or possibly another one of Sarah's employers, compiled the records of the births of Sarah's other children and some of her grandchildren.

Although Sarah Madden never learned to read or write, she was intensely possessive of the documents that she had concerning herself and her family. Although she probably did not remember her mother, Mary Madden, she knew the name, perhaps from having the indenture papers read to her by interested neighbors or employers. The names Mary, Mariah, and Maria, in honor of Mary Madden, were passed down through the Madden family.

The Age of Sarah Madden's Children

Rachael Madden, Daughter of Sarah Madden born March 10th 1776
Voilett Madden daughter of D° born June 12th 1778
David Madden Son of D° born April 21st 1780

Betty Madden daughter of D° born Aug^st 26th 1782
The above Children of Sarah Madden were born agreeable to
the Dates annext to their names.

| A Copy | Francis Madison |
| Test   Wm Banks | Ap 6th 1794 |

Polly Madden Daughter of Sarah Madden, was born March 2nd
    1785
Sarah Madden Daughter of Sarah Madden, was born May 2^d 1787
Fanny Madden, D° of D° was born July the 6th 1789
Nelly Madden, D° of D° was born September the 19th 1793
Nancy Madden, Daughter of Sarah Madden was Born monday
    night the 25th of April 1796
Willis Madden, Son of Sarah Madden, was born [the rest of the
    line is blank, but a partial copy of this list reads "June the _____
    1799"]
Mariah Madden, Daughter of Sarah Madden, was Born monday
    Morning the 22nd of February 1802

[Another list contains:]
Mariah Madden, Daughter of Polly Madden was Born the 26th of
    October 1805
Charity Madden, Daughter of Polly Madden was Born the 12th
    of May 1808
Fanny Madden Daughter of Mariah Madden was born August
    10th 1815
William Madden Son of Mariah Madden was born July 21st 1819

SARAH MADDEN'S ACCOUNT BOOKS

Sarah Madden's account books survive for the last years of the
eighteenth century. After her indenture ended, Sarah earned
her living as a skilled seamstress and laundress. Her customers
included many of the families around the Stevensburg area
and in eastern Culpeper County. Her surviving early account
books show the volume of work that she had to do to support
her family and the many items of eighteenth-century clothing
that she worked on. Also shown are the names of her customers, names that remained familiar to Sarah and her family for
years to come. These account books appear to have been kept
for Sarah by William Banks, a member of a prominent local

family and a partner in the firm of Slaughter & Banks, merchants of Stevensburg. Sarah and her children were kept supplied with food and clothing through the company, in return for Sarah's work on the merchants' and their families' clothes.

[Loose Account Sheets]

Sarah Madden's Accounts   [Pounds, shillings, pence]
1792   Mr. Jo. C. P. Adams

Feby 15th	To one years Wages to date	£ 5. 0. 0.
	To two Shoats at 4 s	0. 8. 0.
	To Ct Soap at 8	0. 4. 0.
	To paid Mr. Waug's George	0. 2. 0.
	To cash paid you	1. 0. 0.
		6.14. 0.

Cr	By stuff for Jacoat & Pettacoate	0.14. 0.
	By Cash receiv'd of you	1. 6. 0.
	By ____ bushels of corn at 12 s	0. 4.10.
	By a Cow & Calf	4.16. 0.
		7. 0.10.
	Bout Down	6.14.
	Ballt Due J.P.A.	6.10.

E.E. P [per] Sarah Mattain

8 days Sarvis over the year	2s. 1.	
to Sope & use of my washing kit	4 9	
	6.10.	

Sary Madden
1792   D^r To Slaughter & Banks

Novr 8	8 yards Stuff @ 1/6	0.12. 0.
1793	3 ditto Linin @ 1/6	0. 3. 0.
April 12	1 7/8 dito ditto @ 1/6	0. 1. 8/4
	1 ditto ditto	0. 1. 0 1/2
	5 ditto ditto	0. 5. 0.

	C^r	
	By Cash at difr tim[e]s	3. 4 1/2
		£ 0.19.4 1/4
	By 2 Busls. Corn @ 4/8	4. 8
	Errs Extd P R. Thom	

APPENDIX ONE

Sarah Madden Acc^t wth
William Banks & Co
Dr Sarah Maddin   In account with William Banks & Co C^r
1796

June 19	To	4 cu brown Sugar 4s.1 meal sifter 2/9 P self		6	9
26		1 quart Whiskey pd.		2	–
27		2 cu Coffee 4/6 1 pair shoes 6/9 P self		11	3
		1 gallon Molasses	5 6	16	9
July 3		1 peck Salt P Sam		1	8
11		1 Bushel Corn rec^d of Mr. Slaughter		5	–
		£	1	12	2

[First account book, ca. 1797–1798]

Reuben Crump   for washing
June 25   To washing a dozen [illegible]
             To making 3 Shirts
       mending 1 jaccoat [jacket] 1/6
       25   mending 6 p^r Stockings 4d. 2/
June 28   to washing 5 pieces
July 5   D^o to 8 pieces
      10   D^o to 6 D^o)
      20   D^o to 6 D^o)
      27   To 3 Pieces   )   Drawd of
Ag^s 6
      19   To 14 Pieces)
Sept   4 Pieces
          12 Pieces
Oct   15 Pieces
          10 Pieces
          14 Ditto
          11 Pieces
          16 Pieces
          11   "
Janry   7 After Christmas   (Reuben Crump, jun^r)
March   27 Pieces Since Christmas
          76 Pieces
Apr   108 Pieces

176

John Crump
To washing 10 Dozen /2
To mending 7 p^r Stocking @ 4d.
To D^o 1/pr Breaches 9d.

Wm Banks Acct. with Sarah Madden
1797
To Makeing 2 winter suits for James
To D^o 2 flanel jaccoats [jackets]
To D^o 2 p^r flanel Draises [dresses]
To D^o 4 p^r Linen Brice James
To D^o 4 Shirts   D^o
1796
To D^o 2 Shirts for James
    D^o 1 Coat
    D^o 1 [illegible]
1797
    D^o 2 p^r Linen Breachings
    D^o 2 Shirts
 96
    D^o 2 Suits for James P Alcock
To making 1 p^r Sheets
     " 2 piller [pillow] Cases
     " 2 flanil jaccoats

	C^r	
To 1 Coffee at 2/3	2	3
1 1/2 Brown Sugar	1	6
12 yds Brown Linon @		
1/6	18	0
7 yd D^o at 1/3	8	9
1 Knife @ 1/6	1	6
Brown thread 6		6
1 Dozen needles 6		6
Rappins 4/	4	0
1 Thimble 3		3
1/2 Sugar 1/6	[illegible]	
	£ 21 3	
1 yd Thread 1/3	1	6
1 quart wiskey 1/6	1	3
1 Sugar 1/3	1	6
	25 1	

Dr William Banks to washing
From 1st Day of January
24th Day of June to washing
16 Dozen 8 1/2 at 4/6 p^r Dozen
June 28 To Washing 8 Pices
July   5 D^o to 26 pieces
       10 D^o to 10 D^o
       20 D^o to 29 D^o
       27 D^o to 22 Pieces
Agst 6)
       15) To 23 Pieces
Aug.   22 Pieces
          40 Pieces
          29 Pieces
          23 Pieces
Oct.   18 Pieces
          61 Pieces
          23 Pieces

Mr. William Banks   washing Ac^t
To making   1 Coat & 1 Pair
Breachs for James
2 Brown Linen Shirts
Sam. 2 Shirts
1 Pair of Sheets for Reubin
1 p^r Draws
3 p^r Breaches
2 Shirts for Sam
2 p^r Breaches

[Second account book, ca. 1799]

To Washing
Mr William Banks
Jan.
1 Crevat
1 Jaccoat
1 pair Stockings
2 Handkercheefs
2 Shirts
2 Crevats
3 p^r Stocking
2 Jaccoats
1 pillercase
2 pocket Hankercheef
17 pieces

Robert Paul
31 pieces

Mr William Banks to making &
mending
March
4 Shirts
3 Crevats
2 pocket Hanker.
2 p^r Stocking
2 flanl jaccoats
1 towel
April
2 or 3 Shirts
4 Crevats
3 p^r Stockings
1 p^r Breeches
1 p^r Draws
2 Handkerchif
1 Suites for James 15s
2 flanel Jaccoats
2 p^r Draws
3 Shirts
3 Crevats 1 week
2 flanel jaccoats

2 towels
2 p^r Stockings
1 Shirt
1 Crevat
1 p^r Stockings
2 Handkercheef
1 p^r Draws
1 p^r Sheets

Mr John Crump D^r to washing
Jan.
7 Shirts
4 Crevats
1 p^r Breeches
1 jaccoat
7 p^r Stocking
3 Shirts
2 p^r Stocking
3 Shirts
Feb.
3 Crevats
3 Handkerchiefs
7p^r Stockings
47 Pieces
February
1 Shirt
1 Crevat
2 p^r Stockings
5 Shirts
March
5 Crevats
5 p^r Stockings
1 p^r Breeches
1 Waiscoat
1 pocket Handkerch.
2 Shirts
2 Crevats
3 p^r Stockings
1 jackoat
Mr J. Crump D^r for washing
4 Shirts
3 Crevats

7 p^r Stockings
1 Handkercheef
2 Shirts
2 Crevats
2 p^r Stockings
April 2 week
4 Shirts
4 Jaccoats
4 Crevats
1 Handkerchif
4 p^r Stockings
May
2 Shirts
2 Crevats
3 p^r Breachs
1 p^r Stockens
1 Handkerchief
1 Shirt
1 Crevat
126 10 Dozen 8 1 / 2

Wm Banks D^r for washing
4 Shirts 2 weeks
3 Crevats
3 p^r Stocking
1 p^r Sheets
1 Towel
1 Handkerchief
1 flanel Jaccoat
 3 week
1 Short
1 Crevat
3 p^r Stockings
1 p^r Breaches
1 p^r Shirts
1 towel
 4 week
2 Shirts
2 Crevats
1 p^r Breeaches
a fla. jaccoat
2 p^r Stockings

2 Handkerchives
1 Towel
1 Towel
   June 1 week
3 Shirts
2 Crevats
2 p^r Breaches
Mr Banks
1 jaccoat
5 p^r Stockings 1 / 2
2 Handkerchief
1 Towel
20 Pieces
   June 4 weeks
11 Pieces
  5

John Crump D^r to mending
to 7 p^r Stockings 24
to 1 p^r Breaches 9

Making for James
4 Breechis
4 Shirts

Mr Reuben Crump D^r to Wash-
ing
Januy   7 6 Shirts
        4 p^r Stocking
Feb^r 1 Hankrchief
        2 Shirts
        1 Shirts
        1 p^r Stockings
Mar   1 Shirt
        2 Shirts
        1 p^r Stockings
        2 jaccoats
        1 Handkerchief
Ap^r 2 Shirts
        1 p^r Stockings
        1 jacoat
   26

        1 Shirt
        1 p^r Stockings
Apr   2 weeks
        2 Shirts
        1 jaccoat
        1 p^r Stockings
        1 Handkerchif
        1 Shirt
        1 p^r Stocking
May   2 Shirts
        1 jaccoat
        2 Stocking   Handkrch
    14

Reuben Crump D^r for washing
   3 week May
1 Shirt
1 jaccoat
3 p^r Stockings
1 Handkerchif
1 Shirt 4 week
1 p^r Breaches
1 jaccoat 5 week
2 p^r Breaches
2 jaccoats
1 p^r Stockings
   June 1 week
1 Shirt
2 jaccoat
1 p^r Breaches
2 p^r Stocking
1 Handkerchi.
   2 week
10 Pieces
   2 weeks
5 Pieces

M[r] James Dicerson D[r] to washing
  At 3 / Dozen
Jan
6 Shirts
2 p[r] Stockings
Febr
2 p[r] Breaches
3 Handkerchiefs
2 Shirts
15 Pieces @ 3 / p[r] D. 3.9

Mar
3 Shirts
3 jaccoats
1 Handkerchief
Apr 2 week
3 Shirts
3 Shirts
4 Shirts
1 p[r] Stocking
2 p[r] Breechs
2 jaccoats
22 Pieces at 3 p[r] D° 6.0
Mending 2 / 8

SARAH MADDEN'S ESTATE RECORDS

Documents for Sarah Madden's inventory and administrator's
account were preserved among the Madden family papers but
were not formally recorded in the Culpeper County court records. The family lived at the old Barnes place through a portion of 1825; by late 1825 Willis Madden had rented a house
elsewhere.

We the undersigned valued twelve head of cattle belonging to
the Estate of Sarah Maddon deceased on the valuation below—

October 7th	One red & white cow & calf	$12.00
	One old red cow	7.00
	One white face cow	9.00
	One short tail cow & calf	10.00
	One dark red heifer	10.00
	One dark red cow buf.	
	[i.e. buffalo, or hornless]	10.00
	Three calf 2.50 each	7.50
	One yearling calf	3.00
	One old black horse	3.00
		$71.50

Armistead Gordon
James A. Gordon
James Turner

APPENDIX ONE

Estate of Sarah Maddon
    To Willis Maddon   D^r

1821	to one pen of Shucks & hauling	$5.00
	paid Colo. Long for pasturage	6.00
	paid Jacob Stout this sum	6.00
1822	paid John S. Wallace for fodder	3.00
	paid Mrs Shakelford for waggon hire	1.00
	paid John Hinshaw for straw	3.00
	paid Thomas Kelly for waggon hire	1.00
	paid Henry Abbott for waggon hire	.66 2/3
1824	paid John Bailey on acct of Daniel Cole	1.00
	paid John Hinshaw	.50
	paid Henry Abbott for waggon hire	.66 2/3
	D° D° D°	.50
	paid Sarah Abbott for daughter Lucy hire	1.50
1825	paid John Bailey	.45
		$29.78 1/3
	to Mr Barnes for Rent	24.00
	to Mr D. Cole	3.00
	to Mr Nall	4.30
	to Mr Gordon	3.50
	to Nancy Madden	5.00
		$69.58 1/3

WILLIS MADDEN RENTS A HOUSE

Willis Madden gave bond for renting a house in 1825 and made subsequent payments to 1830. Probably this was his new living quarters after he left the Barnes farm. The owner of the property, William Lovell, had died, and Martin Nalle was apparently the agent for his estate. John Bailey was another free Negro, and the two families apparently shared the house. Later Willis's relative—possibly brother—Samuel Madden also may have been a tenant.

Know all men by these presents that we Willis Madden and John Bailey are held and firmly bound unto Uriel Terrill, committee of the estate of William Lovell in the just and full sum of forty dollars good and lawful money of Virginia to which payment well and truly to be made we bind ourselves our heirs

182

executors and administrators jointly and severally firmly by these presents. Witness our hands and seals this third day of October one thousand eight hundred and twenty five.

The condition of this obligation is such that whereas Willis Madden and John Bailey have this day rented the tenement now in the possession of Mr. Madison Coleman, now if the above bound shall will and truly pay the just and full sum of Twenty dollars on the fifteenth day of November one thousand Eight Hundred and twenty six and deliver up the tenement at that time then the above obligation to be void otherwise to remain in full force and virtue

his

Teste   WillisX

Jn° Ba [rest torn off]   [rest torn off]

John

Received of Willis Madden this 22d day of Sept[r] 1828 two dollars in part of his Note

M. Nalle

Received 25th March 1830 of Willis Madden five dollars in part of a Note given by Samuel Madden and himself to Charles W. Lovell executor to the Estate of Wm. Lovell dec[d].

Martin Nalle

WILLIS MADDEN'S DEED TO HIS LAND

Willis Madden bought the old Barnes farm from Martin Slaughter by this deed of October 13, 1835 (recorded in Culpeper County Deed Book 2, p. 402).

By January 1841 Willis Madden had paid off the purchase money on his farm. The trustee on the mortgage was also the county clerk, Fayette Mauzy, and he both released the deed of trust and recorded the release (Culpeper County Deed Book 5, p. 193).

At the same time, and on the same page in the deed book, a deed to Willis Madden from William Madden, who was either his brother or his nephew, was recorded. This land was an eighteen-acre tract that William Madden had purchased from Edward Beale a few months before (Deed Book 5, p. 114). The consideration in the transfer was one dollar, indicating that

APPENDIX ONE

Willis was acting as a trustee for the land. Willis transferred the land back to William in September 1865 (Deed Book 16, p. 3). After William's death his son Slaughter Madden sold a portion of the land, which adjoined Lael Church at the town of Lignum (Deed Book 21, p. 432).

Copies of these documents were recorded in the Culpeper County records; the originals were kept by Willis Madden and placed among his family papers.

This Indenture made this 13th day of October 1835 between Martin Slaughter and Martha his wife of the one part and Willis Madden of the other part, witnesseth that for and in consideration of the sum of one dollar by him in hand Madden to them the said Slaughter and wife in hand paid at or before the sealing and delivery of these presents the receipt whereof is hereby acknowledged they the said Martin Slaughter and Martha his wife have bargained and sold and by these presents they do bargain and sell unto the said Madden and his heirs and assigns forever a certain tract or parcel of land lying in the county of Culpeper and containing eighty seven acres be the same more or less, being the same tract mentioned in a deed of conveyance from Stanton Slaughter executor of Robert Slaughter to the said Martin Slaughter bearing date on the 19th day of August 1833 and recorded in the Clerks office of the county court of Culpeper and therein described as the third tract composing the Estate called Grange which was purchased by one Frederick Cline of Robert Slaughter as executor of John Barnes and afterwards conveyed by the said Cline to the said Robert Slaughter in his own right. To have and to hold the said tract or parcel of land unto him the said Madden and his heirs and assigns forever together with all the rights advantages and appurtenances thereunto belonging. And the said Martin Slaughter and Martha his wife for themselves and their heirs the said tract or parcel of land hereby convey and together with all its appurtenances, unto him the said Willis Madden and his heirs and assigns free from the claim or claims of them the said Martin Slaughter and Martha his wife and their heirs and assigns andof all and every person or persons whatsoever, shall, will, and by these presents do forever warrant and defend. In testimony whereof the said Martin Slaughter and Martha his wife have hereunto set their hands and affixed their seals the day and year first written above.

Signed sealed and delivered   Martin Slaughter SEAL
in the presence of   Martha Slaughter SEAL

Culpeper County towit

We Gabriel Gray & J. F. Latham justices of the peace for the county aforesaid in the state of Virginia do hereby certify that Martha Slaughter wife of Martin Slaughter parties to a certain deed bearing date on the 13th day of October 1835 and hereunto annexed personally appeared before us in our county aforesaid and being examined by us privily and apart from her husband and having the said deed fully explained to her, she the said Martha Slaughter acknowledged the same to be her act and deed and declared that she had willingly signed sealed and delivered the same and that she wished not to retract it. Given under our hands and seals this 19th day of October 1835.

Gabriel Gray　SEAL
John F. Latham　SEAL

Culpeper County Court

We Gabriel Gray and John F. Latham justices of the peace for the county aforesaid do hereby certify that Martin Slaughter a party to a certain deed hereto annexed bearing date on the 13th day of October 1835 personally appeared before us in our county aforesaid and acknowledged the same to be his act and deed and desired us to certify his said acknowledgement to the clerk of the county court of Culpeper in order that the same may be recorded. Given under our hands and seals this 19th day of October 1835.

Gabriel Gray　SEAL
John F. Latham　SEAL

1841　Willis Madden—to Clk of Culpeper
　　　　　　　　Dʳ Jany recording deed from Madden　1.50
　　　　　　　　dᵒ　release from Mauzy　　　　　　　1.50
　　　　　　　　　　　　　　　　　　　　　　　　　　3.00

　　　　　　[signed] F. Mauzy

WILLIS MADDEN HELPS A FRIEND AND A RELATIVE, 1844

Robert Hollingsworth, a free Negro living in Cincinnati, wrote in 1844 to ask Willis Madden's help in both obtaining a copy of free papers for Willis's relative Coleman Cowe (Cole) and in being united with his own family.

[To] Mr Wallace Madan   Stevensburg   Culpeper County Va
August the 8th 1844

Dear Sir

I take this oppetunity of riting of a few Lines to inform you that I am well at the present time and hope that you are enjoying the same helth and that I am in Cincinnati and I was talking with Coleman Cowe William Madan nease [nephew?] on friday and he was telling me that he had no free papers else he would come and see you all once more and has rote to Captain Roberts once or twice to get them for him and send them to him but never got no answer from him and I wish you would attend to the [matter] and get them for me and send them to Cincinnati and oblige you faithfull friend and well wisher Direct your letter to Robert E. Hollingsworth & Coleman Coe.

P.S. Sur [Sir] I wish that you would rite to me as soon as you can enquire how all of Connell [Colonel] Thoms people is one and all and give my love to all of them and ask them if they herd any thing of rubin [Reuben] Tthoms having in [any?] of my child[.] he rote me word that I could get it w[h]en I come this fall but I am engage in work so that I cannit come I will come in the spring if I here [hear]. I wish that you would see Betcee and give my Love to her and tell her that I will buy her if she is got no other husband. I told her to wait for me five years in September the 22 1841 I left there would of Come Back but William Miles told me that she was the family way and I thought that if she could be su[i]ted better than I could suit her that she had better suit herself because self situation is better than any other in the world. but when I Come after my child she must not have any objection of my having it when I Come after. Remain your affectionate friend and well wisher answer this letter as soon as possible

Robert E. Hollingsworth

WILLIS MADDEN PETITIONS FOR A ROAD

Willis Madden petitioned the county court for a road and had his request approved, in 1845–1846. Probably the alteration was to move the public road closer to the tavern.

[Culpeper County Minute Book 21]
p. 234 [October 21, 1845] On the motion of Willis Madden for leave to change the road from the Paoli Mills to the Richmond

186

Road where the same runs through the land of the said Madden, ordered that one or more of the comrs [commissioners] of
roads of this county view and report
p. 264 [March 16, 1846] On the petition of Willis Madden for a
road. The report of Chas. Jones one of the road comrs was
returned and ordered to be filed
p. 274 [April 30, 1846] On the petition of Willis Madden for a
road . . . ordered that the road be changed according to the
report of Charles Jones, one of the road comrs.

ENTRIES FROM WILLIS MADDEN'S FAMILY BIBLE

Births, deaths, and marriages were recorded in Willis Madden's family Bible (published by Jesper Harding, 57 South
Third Street, Philadelphia, 1850; sold by Harrold & Murray,
177 Broad Street, Richmond, Virginia). On the flyleaf is written "Willis Madden, 1st Ju[l]y, 1854."

Marriages:
Mr. Adderson R. Bundy and Miss Nansie E. Hurley was mar-
riaed Dec. 23, 1873
Thomas Fields was married to Maria Madden May 6, 1868.

Births:
Kitty Emmer Taylor was Born March 2nd 1853
fountain Taylor Was Born Aug. 26, 1854
Wm. Calvin Taylor was Born Jan. 20, 1856
SuSon Margraiett Taylor Was Born febrary 1st 1858
Mary (Emma) F. Bundy was born Dec. 21st 1874
Margarett Jackson was born April 21 1873
Willis J. Madden was born August 22nd 1862
Thomas O. Madden was born Jan. 26th 1860
Annie J. Madden was born mar. 1865
James Bundy Born sept. 5th 1877
Hannah B. Bundy born Mar. 8, 1880
George W. Bundy was born Sept. 3rd 1882

Deaths:
Thomas Fields died March 18, 1870
Susan M. Taylor Died Mar. 31st 1875
Willis Madden, Sr. died Dec. 1, 1879

APPENDIX ONE

THE DEATH OF WILLIS MADDEN

This letter to T. O. Madden, Sr., from Sadie Madden, daughter of Samuel Madden, was written at the time of Willis Madden's death in 1879. Samuel's wife had apparently been visiting at Maddenville, and Sadie Madden invited her cousin back to the Washington, D.C., area.

[To] Mr Thomas Obed Madden
Tom
    You ask mother to let you come home with her As I want to see you And I think that you can get along very nicely here.
    I was very sorry to hear of the death of Grand Father. I hope you are well my kindest regards to Aunt Maria and Willis.
                                                    From your
                                                    Cousin Sadie

WILLIS MADDEN'S WILL AND THE INVENTORY OF HIS ESTATE

Willis Madden's will was probated on April 19, 1880, and is recorded at Culpeper County Will Book X, p. 416. The inventory, returned to court on May 3, 1880, is recorded at Culpeper County Will Book X, p. 419. (Executor's accounts are recorded at Will Book X, p. 498, and Will Book Y, p. 91.)

    I Willis Madden being of sound mind thanks to Almighty God do make the following declaration that I being at emnity with no man, do "Will" and "Bequeath" the following
vizt. 1st I devize my daughter Maria Fields and my Granddaughter Marguerite Taylor jointly and together my dwelling House, Household Furniture, Orchard, Garden and buildings within the fence with the Land within the fence, the Land known as the Orchard Lot, each of the Above named Maria Fields and Marguerite Tayler their heirs and assigns to own and posses the above mentioned property in equal shares. 2nd I devize the Building known as the African Ebenezar Church, with half (1 / 2) an acre of land surrounding said building to be devoted to the preaching of the Gospel, as long as the colored people will maintain said building to the said purposes, in the event of its

discontinuance, the same to return to my Estate. 3rd I desire that every one of my just and lawful debts be paid out of the residue of my estate not hitherto beqeathed. 4th The Residue of my property to be equally divided between the whole of my Legatees. 5th In the event of the recovery of my claims against the united States I desire all my just and Lawfull before mentioned [debts] to be paid out of the said claims, and not out of the before mentioned property, the balance of said claims after said debts are paid, to be equally divided between the whole of my Legatees. 6th I desire that my son Samuel William Madden will act as Executor of the before mentioned designs, and, carry them out to the full in every respect I further declare that this is my Last Will and Testament whereunto I have set my hand and seal this Eighteenth day of December one thousand eight hundred and seventy two.

his
Willis   X   Madden   SEAL
mark

Witnesses to the above
H. Rollin Lucas
William Hackley

April 29th 1880
We the under signed appraisers of the estate of Willis Madden, Dec. having been duly sworn do find [and] affix the following as the property with its value to wit

One Clock of the value of		$3.00
One cupboard	"	3.50
One Beuro	"	5.00
One "	"	2.50
One Bedstead	"	1.50
Two Beds & Bedding	"	16.00
Ten Chairs	"	2.50
One Table	"	1.25
Two Cows	"	28.00
One Plow	"	3.00

his
Charles R.   X   Doggett
mark

L. D. Philips

his
A. R.   X   Bundy
mark

AN ACCOUNT FROM WILLIS MADDEN'S ESTATE

This portion of the accounting of Willis Madden's estate probably concerned some of the money from Willis's Civil War
claim, which was being held and disbursed by his son Samuel
Madden as executor of the estate.

Culpeper Co. Va. Apr. 20 1880
This is to certify that my father Willis Madden received of S.
W. Madden at different times up to Aug. 28, 1873 the sum of
$180.56 which he witnessed himself. Leaving in bank and in
the hands of S. W. Madden the folering sum $249.64 cents
And since that time Father and I Maria Fields up to his death
Dec. 1st 1879 received cash, groceries & provisions &c to the
amount of $174.75 Making $355.31.

Maria Fields

Witness   Wm Hackley
            T. O. Madden

Appendix Two

PENSION FILE
RECORDS OF
WILLIAM CLARK

ᗡᖳᗡᖳ

*Free Negro and
Revolutionary Soldier*

William Clark's birthplace and parents are unknown. In 1775 or 1776 he enlisted in the revolutionary army and served for the entire term of the six-year war. Although nominally a "soldier servant," he acted as a courier and fought at a number of battles, including Germantown and Monmouth. He was discharged in Philadelphia, Pennsylvania, and then returned home to Virginia.

On March 19, 1785, William Clark received a license to marry Hannah Peters in Stafford County, Virginia. Afterward they moved to Culpeper County. In 1818, aged seventy, he applied for and received a pension for his revolutionary service. He spent his last years as a tenant farmer and farm laborer. He died in eastern Culpeper County on December 8, 1827, a few

APPENDIX TWO

years after his daughter Katherine ("Kitty") married Willis
Madden. Following his death, his widow, Hannah Clark,
applied for a widow's pension, with Willis Madden as her sup-
porting witness.

Culpeper Co. to wit   September Court 1812
   William Clarke came into court and made oath that during
the whole of the Revolutionary War with Great Britain he was
a soldier with the Armies of the United States in the Virginia
line particularly he enlisted with Thomas Wells a Captain in
the 15 Virginia Regiment then under the command of Col° Mason
for three years which time he faithfully Served out and received
a discharge accordingly which discharge he gave in keeping to
Col° John Jameson now deceased and that the said discharge
has not on search been found among Col° Jameson's papers or
any of his representatives that after his term of three years had
expired he Continued in the said Service without intermission
until the end of the War that he was in the quality of a Soldier
Servant under Lieut. Col° Wallace when the troops went to the
succour of Charles Town but that some short time before the
Surrender of that place he was sent by Col° William Heath
express to Virginia by which means he escaped being captured
there but that he still continued in the Service for on his way
back from Virginia he met Col° John Jameson at Wilmington in
North Carolina where he became his Soldier Servant and in
that Capacity waited on him to the State of Connecticutt there
to take Command of a Regiment of Horse and Continued with
him in that Capacity and drew pay as a Soldier to the end of
the War. But now through the Will of Providence it has so
happened that there is not any officer or Soldier now alive within
his knowledge and reach that can prove these facts, and having
lost his discharge as above Stated and having neglected to obtain
any discharge from Col° John Jameson for his latter part he is
left destitute of any possible proof but his own oath. And it was
further proved to the Court by Col° David Jameson that he had
personally heard his brother Col° John Jameson above mentioned speak of the services of the said Clarke during the revolutionary War and that he spoke of him in very high terms and
that he verily believes from what he has heard that he Continued in Service to the end of the War.
                         A Copy Teste
                         Wm. Broadus Clk.

192

State of Virginia
Culpeper Co. to wit

On the sixth day of April 1818 before me the Subscriber one of the Judges of the General Court for the state aforesaid personally did appear William Clarke aged seventy years a resident of the County of Culpeper in the state aforesaid, who being by me first duly sworn, according to law, doth on his Oath make the following declaration in order to obtain the provision made by the late Act of Congress entitled "An Act to provide for certain persons engaged in the land and naval service of the United States in the Revolutionary War." That he the said William Clarke enlisted in 1775 or 1776 in the Continental line of the state of Virginia in the Company commanded by Captain Thomas Wells of the said state and 15 Virg^a Regiment Col^o Mauzy that he continued to serve in the said Corps or in the service of the United States until the close of the War, when he was discharged from the service in Philadelphia state of Pennsylvania—that he was in the Battle of German Town and Monmouth—and that he is in reduced circumstances, and stands in need of the asistance of his Country for support, and that he has no other evidence now in his power of his said services except the transcript of the record and proceedings of the County Court of Culpeper. Sworn to and declared [illegible] the day and year aforesaid

H. Holmes

I Hugh Holmes a Judge of the General Court of the State of Virginia do certify that it appears to my satisfaction that the said William Clark did serve in the Revolutionary Wars stated in the preceeding declaration against the common enemy—and I now transmit the proceedings and testimony taken and had before me to the secretary for the department of War persuant to the directions of the aforementioned act of Congress—
Certified this 6th April 1818 and in my hand there being no seal of Virginia in the court where I preside.

H. Holmes

Virginia Roll
4, 792
William Clarke of Culpeper Co. V^a Private in the Virginia line In the Army of the United States during the Revolutionary War Inscribed on the Roll of Virginia at the rate of 8 Dollars per month, to commence on the 6th of April 1818

Certificate of Pension issued the 8th Dec. 1818 and forwarded
to the Hon. Mr. Strother M.H.R.U.S.
Arrears to the 4th of September 1818 . . . . . .$39.73
Semi-anl all'ce ending March 4 1819. . . . . . . 48. "
Arrs 4 mo 29 / 30
Revolutionary claim
Act 18th March, 1818
Notation sent October 23, 1820
Thomas W. Lightfoot, Fairfax, Virginia

State of Virginia
Culpeper County to wit
  On the 22nd day of August 1820 personally appeared in open
court of record established by an act of the general assembly of
Virginia for the said county William Clarke aged about sixty
four years resident in the said county who being duly sworn
according to law, doth under oath declare that he was enlisted
under Captain Thomas Wells of _____ the 15th Virginia Regiment on the continental line commanded first by Col° James
and afterwards by Col° Edwards and remained in service three
years and more, and in the course of his service was in the
Battles of Monmouth and Germantown—That he hath hereto-
fore made declaration in conformity with the law of the 18th of
March 1818 and that his name is inscribed as a private in the
Army of the Revolution on the pension list roll of the Virginia
Agency at the rate of eight dollars per month to commence on
the 6th day _____ 1818 as will more fully appear by his pension certificate bearing date the 8th day of December 1818 and
signed by J. C. Calhoun Secretary of War with the Seal of State
hereto affixed the number of which certificate appears to be
4792 payable semiannually on the 11th of March at the branch
Bank of the United States at Richmond Virginia—And the said
William Clarke further solemnly swore that he was a resident
citizen of the United States on the 18th day of March 1818 and
that he hath not since that time by gift, sale, or in any manner
disposed of the property or any part thereof with intent thereby
so to diminish it and he being himself within the province of
the act of Congress entitled "An Act to provide for certain persons engaged in the land and naval service of the United States
in the Revolutionary war" passed on the 18th of March 1818
and that he has not nor has any person in trust for him any
property or securities, contract, or debts due to him nor has he

194

any income other than what is contained in the schedule hereto annexed and by him signed.

Sworn to and declared on the 22nd day of August 1820 in open Court before the Justices thereof being in session.

Th. W. Lightfoot Clerk of Court
of the County of Culpeper

Schedule

I William Clarke on the oaths that I have taken do hereby declare the following to be a true list of my property towit
1 horse 25 years old $5.50   one old plough $2
1 Hilling how [hoe] 2 /   1 grubbing Hoe 2 / rake   6 /
And I do further declare that I am a common labourer only, rather infirm and barely able to work—that my family consists of a wife two daughters and a granddaughter—that my two daughters are above the ages of 21 years and at liberty to do as they please and that my Granddaughter is about three years old. And I do further declare that I am in indigent circumstances and stand in need of assistance public or private.

his
William X Clarke
mark

I Thomas Walker Lightfoot Clerk of the Court of the County of Culpeper in the state of Virginia do hereby certify that the foregoing oath and the Schedule thereto annexed are truly copied from the records of the said Court [rest illegible]

[Attached to above]

We William Clark and William Peters acknowledge ourselves held & firmly bound to the commonwealth of Virginia in the sum of L 50 curr. money to the payment whereof to be made to the use of the s^d Commonwealth we bind ourselves our heirs &c firmly to these presents sealed with our seals dated this 19th day of March 1785. The condition of the above obligation is hereby declared to be that whereas on application of s^d Wm Clarke above bound a License hath this day for his marriage with Hannah Peters now if there be no lawful Cause to obstruct the same then the above obligation to be void else of full force & virtue.

William Clark   SEAL
William Peters   SEAL

APPENDIX TWO

Teste [illegible]

Virginia Stafford Co. to wit

The Clerk of the Court of this County in the state aforesaid, I certify the foregoing marriage license of William Clark to be a true copy from the records of my office.

In testimony whereof I hereto set my hand and affix my seal the afsd. County, at the courthouse this 5th day of august 1838, in the 63rd year of the commonwealth

State of Virginia
Culpeper County

This day personally appeared Willis Madden before John Thom a Justice of the Peace in & for the County aforesaid and being first sworn according to law deposeth and sayeth that the within named Hannah Clarke is the Widow of William Clarke dec[d] who drew a pension in his lifetime to the time of his death & that the said William Clarke died on the 8 day of December 1827 & that she never married since his death

his

Willis   X   Madden SEAL

mark

Sworn and subscribed to this the 18 day of August 1838 before me.

John Thom SEAL

I further state I know Willis Madden for many years & believe him to be a man of truth & full confidence may be placed in what he says.

Given under my hand and seal this 18 day of August 1838

John Thom SEAL

Know all men by these presents that I Hannah Clarke widow of William Clarke who was a Soldier in the Revolutionary War do hereby constitute & appoint Charles Allen of Fauquier Co. my true and lawful attorney to assess all or any Compensation which may be due or coming to me from Service Rendered in the Revolutionary War of my deceased husband William Clarke. Given under my hand & Seal this 18 day of August 1838

her

Hannah   X   Clarke SEAL

mark

State of Virginia
Culpeper County
Be it Known that on the 18th day of Augt 1838 before me John Thom a Justice of the Peace for the County aforesaid personally appeared Hannah Clarke above named and acknowledged the aforegoing power of Attorney to Charles Allen. Given from under my hand and Seal this 18th day of August 1838.

John Thom   SEAL

Virginia:
    I Francis T. Lightfoot Clerk of the County Court of Culpeper County in the State aforesaid do hereby certify that John Thom whose name appears on the preceeding certificate is a sworn justice of the peace in and for said County duly commissioned and qualified, and that the foregoing signature purporting to be his is genuine.
    In testimony whereof I have hereafter set my
hand, and affixed the Seal of the said Court
this 23rd day of August 1838, and in the 63rd
year of the Commonwealth

F. T. Lightfoot

[Culpeper County Minute Book 19, p. 124]
Dec. 17, 1838
    A paper writing purporting to be a declaration of Hannah Clarke for a pension, made before John Thom a Justice of the Peace for Culpeper Co., Virginia on the 18th day of August 1838, accompanied by the certificate of the said Thom as to bodily infirmity and credibility of the said Hannah Clarke, at the time said declaration was made before him—also a paper purporting to be an affadavit of Willis Madden, made before the said Justice of the Peace given in the same day and year aforesaid as to the credibility of the said Madden as a witness, were this day presented to the Court, and thereupon the Court doth order that it be certified to the War Department that the said papers were proved to the satisfaction of the Court to be genuine, and entitled to be so regarded to the full extent of their purport. And that it be further certified to the said Department that it was proved to the satisfaction of the court that the said Hannah Clarke did make the declaration in the said paper set forth on the 18th day of August, 1838 before John Thom, who was at the time a duly qualified acting Justice of the peace of the County and state aforesaid—That the said Hannah Clarke

197

at the time of making the said declaration was by bodily infirm-
ity unable to attend Court to make the said declaration, and that
she has always in her neighborhood an excellent character for
honesty and probity—That Willis Madden did make the said
affadivit before the said Justice of the peace on the day and year
aforesaid, and that the said Madden at the time of making the
said affadavit was a man of credit and honesty and his word to
be depended upon.

HANNAH CLARK'S PENSION PAPERS

#1750
Richmond, Virginia

Hannah Clarke
widow of William Clarke
who was a pensioner under the Act of 1818 and who died on
the 8th December 1827 of Culpeper Co. In the State of Virginia
who was a Private in the Company commanded by Captain
Wells of the Regt. commanded by Col. Mason in the Va. line
for 6 years
Inscribed on the Roll of Rich^d Va. at the rate of 80 Dollars —
Cents per annum to commence on the 4th day of March 1836
Certificate of Pension issued the 1st day of Feby 1839 and sent
Chs. Allen   Present
Arrears to the 4th of Sept. 1838 $200.00
Semi-annual allowance ending 4 mar. '39   40.00
                                                    $240.00

Recorded by D. H. Addison, Clerk
Book 9   Vol. 2   page 177

859
Richmond Virginia
Hannah Clarke
widow of William Clarke
who was a Private in the Va. Line for 6 years
Inscribed on the Roll at the rate of 80 Dollars — Cents per
annum, to commence on the 4th day of March, 1843

Certificate of Pension issued the 10th day of July, 1843
and sent to
John Thom
Stevensburg

Culpeper Cty
Va.
ACT OF MARCH 3, 1843
Recorded in Book A
Vol. 1 Page 147

Willis Madden
1848   To the Clerk of Culpeper   Dr.
To be order certifying the heirs of Hannah Clark 44 seals to
pension papers of same 74
                        F. Mauzy $1.18

[Culpeper County Minute Book 22, p. 37]
November 15, 1847
   On the motion of Willis Madden, who qualified and entered
into bond with security according to law, certificate is granted
him to obtain letters of administration upon the estate of Hannah Clarke. decd. The security justified.

[Culpeper County Minute Book 22, p. 436]
September 30, 1852
   Ordered to be certified that it was proved in open court to
the satisfaction of the court that William Clarke was a soldier of
the Revolution in Co¹ John Jameson's troop of Cavalry, that the
said Jameson declared that Clarke was with him both North
and South in the Revolutionary War, that the said Clarke was
a pensioner for revolutionary service by the United States, that
the said Clarke left a widow who was also a pensioner of the
United States for her husband's services aforesaid: that they are
both dead leaving the following children heirs at law of the said
William Clarke, the revolutionary soldier aforesaid, viz. Willis
Clarke, William Clarke, Kitty Madden, Wife of Willis Madden,
who was Kitty Clarke, & Nicholas Clarke.

Appendix Three

CULPEPER COUNTY CENSUS RECORDS

for

The Madden Family

1810–1880

Note: Culpeper Census records for 1790 and 1800 no longer survive.

1810 CENSUS

The three Madden households in Culpeper County in 1810 were those of Sarah Madden ["Sr."] and her daughters Polly and young Sarah ["Jr."]. The four free Negroes in Polly's household would have been herself, her children Mariah and Charity, and another child or sibling. Young Sarah also had several children by this time. The five free Negroes in old Sarah's family probably would have been herself and her four youngest children: Nelly, Nancy, Willis, and Mariah. Sarah's other daughters, Betty and Fanny, may have been living in other households or may have left the area by this time.

MADDEN FAMILY CENSUS RECORDS

1810 Census, Culpeper County [p. 27]
Polly Madden   4 Free Negroes in Household
Sarah Madden, Jr.   3 Free Negroes in Household
Sarah Madden, Sr.   5 Free Negroes in Household

1820 CENSUS

In the 1820 Census of Culpeper County, old Sarah and her
daughters Polly and Sarah (Sally) were still the only three
Madden households in the county. Polly now had a total of
four children; young Sarah had seven. Old Sarah's family consisted of herself (female over forty-five), Willis (male under
twenty-six), two young women under the age of twenty-six
(probably Sarah's youngest daughters Mariah and Nancy). Two
of the children under age fourteen may be Fanny and William,
Mariah's children; the others may be Nancy's oldest children.

1820 Census, Culpeper County [p. 87]
Polly Madden   1 Free Colored Male under 14
                       3 Free Colored Females under 14
                       1 Free Colored Female under 45

Sally Madden   4 Free Colored Males under 14
                       3 Free Colored Females under 14
                       1 Free Colored Female under 45

Sarah Madden   2 Free Colored Males under 14
                       1 Free Colored Male under 26
                       2 Free Colored Females under 14
                       2 Free Colored Females under 26
                       1 Free Colored Female over 45

1830 CENSUS

Willis Madden was apparently living in another household, of
which he was not the head, during the 1830 Census. Of the
two Madden households listed in that census, Nancy Madden,
of course, was Willis's sister; the five children in her household
may have all been hers, or some may have been orphans of her

dead sister Sarah. The identity of Samuel Madden is unknown. He would have to have been born between 1775 and 1794 and would have been too old to be one of old Sarah's grandchildren. Possibly he was a son whose birth was not recorded among those of Sarah's other children. There are references to a "Sam" and "Sam Madden" in Sarah's account books, in the affidavit of William S. Jones in 1823 and in Willis Madden's early business receipts. Willis Madden named one of his sons Samuel (born in the early 1820s), suggesting that this was a family name.

1830 Census, Culpeper County
[p. 89]
Nancy Madden 1 Free Colored Male under 10
  1 Free Colored Male between 10 and 24
  1 Free Colored Female under 10
  2 Free Colored Females between 10 and 24
  1 Free Colored Female between 24 and 36

[p. 151]
Samuel Madden 2 Free Colored Males under 10
  1 Free Colored Male between 36 and 55
  1 Free Colored Female between 24 and 36

1840 CENSUS

By 1840 Willis Madden, now a landowner, was head of his own household. Nancy and Polly were his sisters; Maria was probably his niece of that name. The identity of William Madden is not documented. He may be the "Billy" referred to in several of the Madden documents. According to the 1850 Census, he would have been born around 1800, so would have been of an age to be either a nephew to Willis Madden or a younger brother unrecorded in the family birth records.

1840 Census, Culpeper County [p. 259]
Polly Madden (Free Negro) 1 Male between 10 and 24
  1 Female under 10
  2 Females between 10 and 24
  1 Female between 24 and 36
  1 Female between 55 and 100

MADDEN FAMILY CENSUS RECORDS

Maria Madden (Free Negro)   1 Male between 10 and 24
1 Female under 10
2 Females under 10
1 Female between 24 and 36

Nancy Madden (Free Negro)   2 Males under 10
1 Male beween 10 and 24
2 Females under 10
3 Females between 10 and 24
1 Female between 36 and 55

Willis Madden (Free Negro)   1 Male under 10
3 Males beween 10 and 24
1 Male between 36 and 55
3 Females under 10
1 Female between 36 and 55
1 Female between 55 and 100

(Hannah Clark, aged 87, a Revolutionary Pensioner, living in this household)

William Madden (Free Negro)   1 Male between 36 and 55
1 Female under 10

1850 CENSUS

The 1850 Census was the first in which the name of every member of a household was given. There were half a dozen Madden households in Culpeper then, all descendants of Sarah Madden. For reference, the census information on related families is included.

French Madden (Census, p. 226) was a son of Willis and Kitty. Fanny Madden (p. 232) was apparently Willis's niece of that name, daughter of his youngest sister, Maria; according to the family birth records, Fanny was born in 1815, not the ca. 1810 given in the census.

The parents of William and Burgess Madden (pp. 233 and 238) are uncertain, but at ten years old, they were of an age to be grandsons or great-grandsons of old Sarah. From her age Mary Madden (p. 245) would be a granddaughter of Sarah, probably, from the data in the 1840 Census, a daughter of

Polly or Nancy Madden. Maria Madden (p. 248) was the daughter of Polly Madden, Willis's sister (see the family birth records). William Madden (p. 248) was either the brother or nephew of Willis Madden (see 1840 Census). Nancy Madden (p. 248) was one of Willis's older sisters.

In Willis's household (p. 249), William Clark was Kitty's brother; Samuel and William were apparently Willis's nephews, sons of Fanny Madden Hackley. Of Willis and Kitty's children, French Madden (p. 226), the millwright was living elsewhere; Samuel and Margretta had already left Culpeper County.

Lucy Madden (p. 251) was of the right age to be another granddaughter of old Sarah; she was probably a daughter of young Sarah or Polly. Maria Madden Bannister (p. 260) was the youngest daughter of old Sarah and had long since established a household with Christopher Bannister and become known by that surname.

Of old Sarah's children, only Willis, Nancy, and Maria are known to have been still living in Culpeper. The other children had died or left the area by then.

1850 Census, Culpeper County

[p. 226]

French Madden, 25, mulatto male, millwright, living with the household of Charles Jones and family (white)

[p. 232]

Fanny Madden, 40, black female
Eliza Madden, 22, black female
Washington Madden, 2, black male
Lucy Madden, 1, black female
all living in the household of George Balthis, blacksmith

[p. 233]

William Madden, 10, black male, living in the household of John Worlledge, farmer

[p. 238]

Burgess Madden, 10, black male, living in household of Coleman Shackelford, farmer

[p. 245]

Mary Madden, 26, black female (Head of Household)
Strother Madden, 4, black male

MADDEN FAMILY CENSUS RECORDS

Mary Madden, 3, black female
John Madden, 1, black male
[p. 248]
Maria Madden, 45, mulatto female (Head of Household)
Milly Madden, 17, mulatto female
Mary Madden, 16, mulatto female
Daniel Madden, 12, mulatto male
Richard Madden, 9, mulatto male
Robert Madden, 8, mulatto male
William Madden, 4, mulatto male
[p. 248]
William Madden, 50, mulatto male, laborer (Head of House-
   hold)
Susan Cole, 35, female mulatto
Slaughter Madden, 7, mulatto male
Jane Madden, 7 months, mulatto female
[p. 248]
Nancy Madden, 55, mulatto female (Head of Household)
Ann Madden, 32, mulatto female
Sarah M. Madden, 22, mulatto female
John Madden, 21, mulatto male
William P. Madden, 16, mulatto male
Bernard Madden, 4, mulatto male
Farley Madden, 2, mulatto male
Nancy Madden, 6 months, mulatto female
[p. 249]
Willis Madden, 51, black male, farmer (Head of Household)
Kitty Madden, 50, mulatto female
Coleman Madden, 23, mulatto male
Sarah A. Madden, 18, mulatto female
Mary F. Madden, 16, mulatto female
Maria Madden, 12, mulatto female
Jack Madden, 10, mulatto male
Nathaniel Madden, 8, mulatto male
William Clark, 60, mulatto male, laborer
Samuel Hackley, 40 black male, laborer
William Hackley, 30, mulatto male, laborer
[p. 251]
Lucy Madden, 38, mulatto female (Head of Household)
Elizabeth Madden, 21, mulatto female
James Madden, 12, mulatto male

Martha Madden, 9, mulatto female
Granville Madden, 5, mulatto male
William Madden, 6 months, mulatto male
Mary G. Madden, 4 months, mulatto female
William H. Madden, 30, mulatto Male, laborer
[p. 260]
Chris. Bannister, 50, mulatto male, farmer (Head of House-
 hold)
Maria Bannister, 49, mulatto female
Jane Bannister, 19, mulatto female
Kitty Bannister, 13, mulatto female
John P. Bannister, 11, mulatto male
Edmonia Bannister, 9, mulatto female
Albert Bannister, 7, mulatto male
William Hollinger, 16, mulatto male, laborer

1860 CENSUS:
Households of Willis Madden and Maria Madden

This census was taken in mid-1860. Kitty Madden had died a
few months before, and only Willis's son Jack was still at home.
Maria was living nearby with her infant son, Thomas Obed
Madden; the identity of the six-year-old Mary Madden living
with her is uncertain.

1860 Census, Culpeper County
[p. 849]
Maria Madden, 24, mulatto female
Thomas O. Madden, 7 months, mulatto male
Mary Madden, 6, mulatto female
[p. 849]
Willis Madden, 61, black male, farmer (owns $1180.00 of real
 estate)
Jack Madden, 20, black male

1870 CENSUS:
Willis Madden's Household

By 1870 Willis Madden's household consisted of himself, his
widowed daughter Maria Madden Fields, Maria's two sons,

Willis's granddaughter Margaret (also known as Marguerite) and another young relative.

1870 Census, Culpeper County
Stevensburg District [p. 7]
Willis Madden, 70, male, farmer (owns $1044.00 of real estate)
Maria Fields, 36, female, keeping house
Willis Jackson Madden, 7, male
Thomas Obit Madden, 9, male
Margarett Taylor, 12, female
Nancy Herley, 15, female
(all members of this and the surrounding households appear to be listed as white in this Census)

1880 CENSUS:
Maria Madden Fields's Household

Following Willis Madden's death in 1879, Maria Madden Fields became head of a household made up of herself, her two sons, and a boy who worked on the farm.

1880 Census, Culpeper County
Stevensburg District [p. 21]
Maria Fields, 43, black female, keeping house and farming
Thomas O. Madden, 20, black male, son, works on farm
W. J. Madden, 17, black male, son, works on farm
Richard Brooks, 13, black male, servant, works on farm

INDEX

italicized page numbers refer to illustrations and captions

INDEX

Calhoun, John C., 194
Campbell, David, 161
Carter, Mable, 136, 137
Catholic Church, 163–64
Cedar Mountain, Battle of, 101, *102*
census data:
  1790, xiii
  1810, 46, 200–201
  1820, 201
  1830, 46, 201–2
  1840, 202–3
  1850, 90–91, 203–6
  1860, 206
  1870, 206–7
  1880, 207
Chinquapin Neck, 71
civil rights movement, 166
Civil War, xix–xx, 98–100
  artifacts left on Madden farm, *112*
  Borcke's visit to Madden's tavern,
    103–6
  Brandy Station, Battle of, *106*, 107
  Cedar Mountain, Battle of, 101, *102*
  Culpeper County battles, 101, 106–
    8
  devastation of countryside, 101,
    108–10, *109*, *110*
  Madden farm, impact on, 98, 108–
    10
  map of Rapidan region, *99*
  reimbursement to Maddens for
    losses incurred, *118*, 120–21
  stragglers, 102
  union camps, *108*
Clark, Hannah Peters, 59, 88, 191,
    192, 196, 197–99
Clark, Nicholas, 199
Clark, William (elder), 43, 48, 59
  pension records, 191–99
Clark, William (younger), 90, 91
Cline, Frederick, 64, 184
clock owned by Willis Madden, 92–
    93, *92*
Cole, Daniel, 57
Coleman, Madison, 60
Coleman, W. A., 121

Collins, James, 3
Collins, Joseph, 3
colonization of free Negroes, xvi
common-law relationships, 36
credit, 84, *85*, 142
crossroads, 69, 71
Crump, John, 30, 177, 179, 180
Crump, Reuben, 26, 30, 32, 176, 180
Culpeper County, Va., 27–28
  Civil War battles, 101, 106–8
  sections of, 111–12

Daingerfield family, 160
dairy businesses:
  of Sarah Madden, 38, 41, 45
  of T. O. Madden, Jr., 156, 157–59
Davis, Jack, 119
debt:
  T. O. Madden's opposition to, 141–
    42
  treatment of debtors (1700s), 11–12
Dicerson, James, 34, 181
Doggett, Charles R., 189
Doggett, Mary, 139
Doggett family, 161
Douglass, Frederick, 142
Downman, Joseph, 44
Dred Scott v. Sandford (1857), xvii

Ebenezer Baptist Church building,
    119, 188
education:
  children of T. O. Madden, xxi,
    128–29, 143–44, 147, 153
  children of T. O. Madden, Jr.,
    162–64
  children of Willis Madden, 95–96
  free Negroes and, xix
  Negro schools (post–Civil War), xx–
    xxi, 117, 119
  school trustees, 138–39
  teacher's life, xx–xxi, 126–28, 130–
    32, 136–39, 144
  vocational education for Negroes,
    40–41, 73
Episcopal Church, 44

210

INDEX

INDEX

INDEX

Madison, Col. James, 11–12, *16*, 18, 20
  home of, 13–15, *13*, *15*
  will of, 23
Madison, James, Jr., 15, 23, 167
Madison, Nelly, 15
Madison, Nelly Conway, 15, *16*
Madison, Sarah, 15
Madison, William, 15
Madison, v. Fraser's Executrix, 12
marriage by free Negroes, xviii–xix, 36
Marshall, Aleck, 122
Marye, John L., Jr., 122
Mason, Julia, 135
Mauzy, Fayette, 183, 199
Meade, Gen. George G., *108*
Mercer, James, xiv, 20–21
Miles, William, 186
Montpelier (Madison estate), 13–15, *13*, *15*
Mount Pony Baptist Meetinghouse, 45, 47
mulatto children:
  indentured servitude for, 17–18
  laws concerning, x–xi, 1–2
  treatment in colonial period, xxviii–xxx
Myrtle family, 159

Nalle, Martin, 182, 183
National Geographic, 167
"Negro," use of word, xxv

Orange, Va., 13
Orange and Alexandria Railroad, 94
oxen, 159–60

Page, Frances, 133
panic of 1893, 142
Paul, Robert, 178
Paul, William, 61
paupers, assistance for, xxvii–xxviii, 3, 4
Payne, Johnny, 136
Pelham, Maj. John, 103, 104–6, *105*

Pennsylvania, laws concerning Negroes, 23
pensions:
  for revolutionary veterans, 43, 191–99
  for teachers, 144
Peters, William, 195
petitions to county government, 88, 186–87
Philips, L. D., 189
Phillips, Lawrence, 126
Phillips, Odenla Madden ("Denny"), 56, 128, 133, 143, 147, *149*, 152, 161
Pittsburgh, Pa., 125
Pleasonton, Gen. Alfred, *106*
Pope, Gen. John, *102*
Prospect Hill (Madison estate), 18, *18*, 23–24
Prosser, Gabriel, xvi

Quakers, 28

railroads, 94
Rapidan River, *17*
Redd, Seth W., 96
Redd, William, 95, *96*
Rees, J. D., 87
Rees, Thomas, Jr., 87
Revolutionary War pensions, 43, 191–99
Reynolds, Annie, 157
Richards, James, 82
roads, petitions for, 88, 186–87
Ross, Peter, 144, 161
Ross, William B., 81
Russell, John H., xii*n*, xiii*n*, xiv*n*, xvi*n*, xvii*n*, xix*n*

school trustees, 138–39
Scott, French & Co., 84
seamstress-laundress work, 14, 26–27, 28–32, 34–35, 38, 41
segregation, 152, 164–66
Semple, John, 7

INDEX